To Pam

Lots o'...

&

Best Wishes

Paul x

Very Much Alive

BY PAUL JAMESON

Very Much Alive

PAUL JAMESON

StoryTerrace

Text Johnny Acton, on behalf of StoryTerrace
Design Mitar Stjepcevic, on behalf of StoryTerrace
Copyright © Paul Jameson
First print June 2022

StoryTerrace

www.StoryTerrace.com

CONTENTS

DEDICATION	7
FOREWORD	9
INTRODUCTION - THE ARIA	15
1. THE 'BEFORE' SHOT	19
2. DIAGNOSIS	45
3. THE GRIM REAPER	55
4. BUCKET LIST ONE: ADVENTURES (PART ONE)	63
5. BUCKET LIST ONE – ADVENTURES (PART TWO)	87
6. PAUL'S ARIA – A STRANGE TALE	125
7. EMOTIONAL BUCKET LIST	139
8. THE BIRTH OF AURA	157

9. LOVE, LAUGHTER, GENEROSITY AND KINDNESS	173
10. ASSISTED DYING	191
11. MY BATTLE WITH MND	199
12. THE LAST BIG TABOO	209
EPILOGUE: THE ROAD AHEAD	217

DEDICATION

This book is dedicated to my gorgeous wife Jess and three wonderful children, David, Jo and Rosie. It's also dedicated to my mother Shirley for her unwavering support over 62 years - it can't have been easy at times!

I love you all dearly.

FOREWORD

My name is Paul Jameson, and I'm a 62-year-old family man from Surrey. You've probably never heard of me. But I have a story to tell that is relevant to everyone. This is because it deals with something we all have to face sooner or later, even though we'd much rather not. That 'something' is our mortality, and I think I've got an interesting take on it.

On 12th June 2017, I received a terrifying diagnosis: Motor Neurone Disease (MND), or ALS as it is known in the US, which is a terminal disease. (You may remember the Ice Bucket Challenge a few years ago that raised $115 million for ALS research.) In layman's terms, MND affects the nerves that control the muscles in your body, which progressively stop responding to what your brain is asking them to do and eventually waste away. The disease usually affects the limbs first, then the mouth region. For me, it was the other way around. I now cannot talk, as my tongue and lips can no longer move. I also have difficulty swallowing and eating.

I look at pictures of people with advanced MND sitting in wheelchairs. They have an oxygen mask on to breathe, a feeding tube in their stomach, their head lolling to one side because their neck muscles cannot support the weight of their head. Their bodies are lifeless and wasted away. I shudder, as I'm looking at my future.

Nobody seems to know why you get MND, how to treat it or what the likely progression is, let alone find a cure. MND is a rare disease, and as such, it isn't commercially viable for pharmaceutical companies to invest in finding drugs that will control the symptoms. For a long time, MND was the forgotten illness, a condition nobody seemed to care about. In the Autumn 2021 budget, a campaign by the MND Association and other charities for the UK government to include an extra £50 million in funding for vital research was ignored by Chancellor of the Exchequer Rishi Sunak in the spending review. However, following constant pressure from the MND Association and other groups and charities, Prime Minister Boris Johnson intervened, and the £50 million funding was approved on 14th November. At last, there was something to celebrate in the MND community, giving us a much-needed sense of hope and optimism.

Up until my diagnosis, I'd led a quite unremarkable life. I'd been fairly average at most things – not academically gifted, jack of many sports but master of none, reasonably successful in business but not massively so. Nevertheless, I had always felt lucky and knew that I had lived a privileged life. I was born into a close and hugely supportive middle-class family in Surrey, had a very happy childhood and was well-educated. Now I had a comfortable family home, a lovely wife and three great kids. Plus a few animals and regular holidays.

It was when I got my MND diagnosis that my life became more remarkable. I was told that my life expectancy was two years, and there was no cure. Nothing like that for focusing the mind!

This book mainly concentrates on the years after I was told I was dying and why they have been some of the best I've ever had. My diagnosis has taught me how to live, not die. It's changed my perspective on so many things. It has made me realise what's important in life, brought me closer to family and friends, set me new challenges and provided me with many new opportunities. So, this is not a biography of my whole life. Instead, it focuses on the more interesting and eventful post-diagnosis part of it.

This book also explains why, in late 2019, I set up a business called Aura (aura.life), which helps people prepare for and manage their deaths in a better way. It enables them to leave a lasting legacy and seeks to open up the conversation around death and dying. The business is now beginning to flourish.

I'm not asking you to agree with anything I write in this book. What I can promise you is that I say it as I see it. I'm merely describing how I feel about things and how they have worked out for me. I'm not trying to preach my beliefs and philosophies, just, for better or worse, to tell you what they are. They may resonate with you, or they may not.

VERY MUCH ALIVE

I do hope, however, that this book will help and inspire people who have difficulties in life, whether they are health scares, life-limiting illnesses or mental health issues. And does the trick for anyone who just wants something uplifting and positive to read. I have learned so much in the last five years, and I want to share my story, as I believe many people will benefit from it.

I've tried to make this an easy read, an enjoyable page-turner with plenty of humour. But it does embrace a subject that we find difficult in this country and handle needlessly badly. That subject is death. It's not as if only the unlucky ones die. We all have a terminal illness from the day we're born. It's called 'life'.

Fortunately, attitudes are beginning to change, and part of what I've set out to do is to explore those changes. I've read many books on the subject of death and dying, and several passages from them are quoted here. They all have one thing in common: a potentially game-changing understanding that knowing you're going to die can be a happy and peaceful time, fulfilling and rewarding. Embracing death, planning for it and discussing it, really can help you live a fuller, richer life.

This has certainly been true for me. Over the last five years, I've reached a state of contentment, inner peace and happiness that I've never had before. This phenomenon is far from unique to me – many people who are about to die experience the same feelings, as I know through engaging

VERY MUCH ALIVE

with thousands of others who are in the same boat as me. Why exactly is this? In the course of this book, I'll try to provide some answers.

INTRODUCTION - THE ARIA

'You have to seek the wonderful in life, it won't come knocking at your door.'
Rob Burrow, *Too Much to Live For*

September 2021. The scene: the Snape Maltings in Suffolk. The original purpose of this magnificent building – the malting of barley for the brewing industry – was much more up my usual street than its current function, which is serving as the home of the annual Aldeburgh Music Festival, founded by the legendary composer Benjamin Britten.

The occasion: a performance of Sound Voice, a visionary exploration of the human voice and possibilities of collaboration.

The performer (one among many): a tall, very nervous, tone-deaf 61-year-old who has never sung in front of a paying audience in his life.

The reason I am here is to sing an aria. For those who don't know (and I was no opera buff before the unlikely chain of events that led me here), an aria is a self-contained piece of music, usually for one voice. But on this occasion, there will be two performers, for reasons that will become apparent: myself and a professional opera singer called Marcus Farnworth.

The aria in question is called 'Paul', appropriately enough. The music has been written by the wonderful composer Hannah Conway and the words by the equally excellent lyricist Hazel Gould. It is based on six hours of Zoom interviews they have conducted with me during lockdown. The theme is what my voice means to me. Actually, though, it's a kind of love song to my wife, Jess, who is sitting in the audience alongside my mother, Shirley, and two sisters, Sally and Juliet. This was perceptively pointed out by Roddy Williams, the baritone who accompanied me the previous time I performed the aria on stage. I guess it was obvious from the line, 'Can you hear how much I love you, how much I always will?' It makes me cry just typing that, but then I cry very easily these days.

So, I was misleading you if I implied that I'd never sung the aria before in public. But on that occasion, there had been no strangers in the audience, just Jess and our son David. Nevertheless, it had still been pretty daunting, as the venue was the London Coliseum. 'You haven't really done any singing or performance before, have you?' Hannah had asked me from her piano stool. 'So this is quite a good place to start, really, on the main stage of the English National Opera.' It had been a wonderful experience, which had left me in tears of joy. 'My name is Paul Jameson, and I'm in total happiness,' I had said afterwards in an interview with the BBC, which was covering the story for a breakfast news feature. But at the Coliseum, I'd had the lines of the aria fed to me. This time, I've had to memorise them.

I can't say I cover myself in glory. I fluff the final words, which should be 'I know this is my voice, and it sounds to me like my life and soul', but they come out as something else entirely. Fortunately, I don't think too many people notice. They give us a standing ovation at the end, and we have to do a curtain bow. This is very gratifying, of course, but it's also totally surreal. How on earth did I end up singing an aria to a paying audience when I have MND? I have very little voice left and struggle to walk, let alone sing . . .

Read on, and I'll tell you!

1

THE 'BEFORE' SHOT

'Death is the sound of distant thunder at a picnic.'
W.H. Auden

If I had never developed MND, I don't think I'd be bothering you with my life story. Don't get me wrong; plenty of things had happened to me over the previous 57 years, and obviously, they had meant a great deal to me. But they weren't what you'd call earth-shattering. In a way, though, that's precisely why I think it's important to give you an idea of my backstory. What happened to me could happen to literally anyone. I'd go further, in fact. MND itself is extremely rare, but the predicament it has placed me in – having to face the prospect of my own death – is absolutely guaranteed to happen to everyone. They may not get as much warning as me – they may be killed by a sudden heart attack or fall under the proverbial bus – but they're definitely going to die at some point. And that goes for you, the people you love and even Keith Richards.

VERY MUCH ALIVE

You may choose to decide not to think about this uncomfortable fact. I know I didn't before I received my diagnosis. It's an understandable position to take, and I wouldn't want to deprive anyone of that right. But I am here to offer a different perspective. And to explain how I came to see things the way I do now, I need to give you some idea of what kind of person I was before all this happened to me.

*

Let me begin with a story. One day in December 2015, I woke up with a terrible hangover. There was something I urgently needed to do, but what on earth was it? Then I remembered. I was supposed to let my daughter Rosie's beautiful thoroughbred horse, Hilly, out of her stable.

Rosie and my wife, Jess, had gone to Paris for the weekend to do some Christmas shopping, leaving me in charge of Hilly. I had just two tasks to perform: put her in the stable at night and let her out into her field in the morning. Simple enough, you'd have thought.

The problem was that the day before I had taken part in an annual ritual. Every year, in the run up to Christmas, me and three old friends meet up for lunch. A long and very liquid lunch. We usually go to the Skylon restaurant in the Royal Festival Hall, overlooking the Thames. The other protagonists are Chris Guinness, Tim Draper and Tony Brampton.

I met Chris at school when I was 14, and we've been great mates ever since. He is an extremely loyal and generous friend, and I love him to bits. Tim and I worked together in Covent Garden when I was doing a placement from university. (OK, it was technically a polytechnic in those days, but who cares?) We had three things in common: drinking, smoking and living in Parsons Green. Every day after work, we'd walk down to Embankment tube station, dropping in on a few pubs en route, and wait for a District Line train to take us home. But we were delighted if a Circle Line train came first because this meant we could jump out at Sloane Square for another quick drink. There used to be a bar on the platform, conveniently positioned opposite the smoking carriage, and we had enough time to down a whisky before the right train came along. If it was preceded by another Circle Line train, happy days! This meant another high-speed round. Tony was, and still is, a great mate of Tim – like Chris and I, they met at school. The four of us shared many happy memories in our 20s, including making a shocking movie called Martin. Actually, let's not go there.

The Christmas lunch in 2015 was very like the others: copious bottles of red wine followed by one or two Kummels (a great digestive, if you haven't tried it). As ever, we had great fun. The drawback was that by the time I got home, it had already been dark for three hours, and my horse management skills weren't necessarily at their sharpest. I seemed to recall just about getting Hilly into her stable, but I couldn't be entirely sure.

VERY MUCH ALIVE

Next morning, I dragged myself out of bed and headed out into the cold fog to find out. Out of the corner of my eye, I saw something moving to the left of our house. To my horror, I realised it was Hilly. She had fallen into a deep ditch and was desperately struggling to get out. But it wasn't working. Oh fuck, I thought; I must have left the stable door open.

Cursing myself for being so stupid, I raced over and jumped into the ditch. I pushed and pushed, but it was no good – the horse's legs were hopelessly stuck in the mud. Then things got a whole lot worse. Hilly suddenly keeled over and fell on top of me. Now I was pinned in a freezing ditch by half a tonne of dead horse.

I wouldn't say my whole life flashed before me at this point, but it certainly caved in. Rosie would never forgive me for this, and my wife was probably going to divorce me if I survived. But that wasn't a given because I was finding it increasingly difficult to breathe. Is this how my story ends? I wondered. It wasn't the kind of death I'd have wanted for myself.

Fortunately, my son David, who was asleep in an upstairs room not too far from the ditch, must have heard my muffled cries for help because he burst onto the scene and started jumping up and down on the lifeless animal. His intentions were good – he was attempting CPR – but the added weight was really not what I needed in my current predicament. 'David, please stop doing that. The horse is most definitely dead,' I wheezed out to him.

In the end, he managed to haul me out from under the horse. Once I was free, my first instinct was to face the music, so while I sat on the edge of the ditch gasping, David went to get my phone so I could break the awful news to my wife and daughter in Paris. Jess was very calm and practical, as usual, and told me to call the vet and knacker. But poor Rosie was in floods of tears. They said they'd catch the next train home.

As we walked back to the house, I was distraught. But then David nudged me and pointed to the stable. 'Er, Dad . . .,' he said. There, quietly munching her hay, was Hilly, in her stable. WT actual F?!? Then I took another look at the horse in the ditch. It had the same kind of red rug on its back as Hilly, but come to think of it, it did look a bit different from her.

I immediately called Paris with the wonderful news that I'd got the wrong horse. The dead one belonged to a neighbour. The poor animal had escaped from its stable, wandered onto our property and got into fatal trouble. Rosie was overjoyed, though obviously full of sympathy for the owner. I just breathed a huge sigh of relief.

The reason I'm telling you the story of this debacle right at the beginning of this book is that it neatly encapsulates the way I live. I get myself into trouble, then I find a way out of it and come up smiling. I just act on instinct, without thinking too much. Like anyone else, I have my emotional highs and lows, but I'm fundamentally a lucky person. That horse could have been Hilly. Alternatively, if I had been one foot to the right when it fell on me, I would have been crushed to death. But neither of those things happened. One day, of course, I won't be so lucky. There's a fine line between life and death, and none of us can stave off the latter forever. But as I've increasingly come to realise, that needn't be a problem.

Receiving a terminal diagnosis hasn't changed the way I think about things. What it has done is make me more determined than ever to live life to the full. I can honestly say that the past few years have been among the happiest and most fulfilling I've ever had, and I'm looking forward to the future, whatever it brings. I think we, as a society, have got it badly wrong about death, just like I was wrong about the horse in the ditch. Approached in the right way, the knowledge that our time here is limited can be the most life-enhancing thing there is.

*

I was born in April 1960. My mother tells me it was a sunny day, and I was a sunny little boy. But I was also quite a handful (my family and friends will tell you that hasn't changed!). Mum used to have to cage me into my pram with bamboo to prevent me from climbing out of it, and she often felt compelled to leave me at the bottom of the garden so the noise from the nearby road would drown out my screams.

VERY MUCH ALIVE

Other choice episodes from my infancy include me raiding my father's wallet and cutting the five-pound notes in it into tiny pieces (they were worth about £100 each in today's money). Then I moved on to his collection of ties and gave them the same treatment. On another occasion, he was foolish enough to leave me in his Jaguar while he popped into a shop. 'I wonder what would happen if I pushed the button on that lever thing?' I asked myself. So, I let off the handbrake, and the car ploughed straight into the shop. Then there was the time I climbed up a slide in a busy toy shop, dropped my shorts and peed down the chute . . .

Clearly, I could be hard work, but I had a very happy childhood. It wasn't all plain sailing – I spent my fourth birthday in hospital with encephalitis – but on the whole, I led a thoroughly privileged existence. My father, David, had founded a successful electronics component business called Waycom, and we had the lifestyle to match. For my first six years, we – my dad, my mother, Shirley, my older sister Sally (b. 1958) and my younger siblings Andrew and Juliet (b. 1963 and 1966 respectively) – lived in Chipstead in Surrey, which wasn't exactly deprived. Then we traded up to Updown House in Chobham. My father, who was a fanatical swimmer, built a pool in the garden. He was very entrepreneurial and developed a system using polystyrene segments for creating a lane within it that he could use in winter while leaving the rest of the pool covered.

VERY MUCH ALIVE

I continued to be naughty when I went to Fare Dene Nursery School – I got into big trouble with a couple of girls called Tracey and Trudy, though I swear to this day that it wasn't my fault – but I have fond memories of the place. When I was six, I moved on to a local day prep school, which I loved. I was very keen on sport, even though I didn't excel at any particular one. What I enjoyed was the physical exertion, the friendships I made and the shared experiences. Sport has remained a huge part of my life, both participating in it and watching it. (You'll have to forgive me but I'm an avid Chelsea fan. My father took me to my first match at Stamford Bridge in 1972, and after that, I was hooked.) It's how I get my highs.

Academically, I was OK, but nothing to write home about. Still, I managed to get into a top public school, Wellington College, when I was 13, which was a huge privilege. I got off to a good start – during my first year I was in the 'A' stream and the rugby first XV for my age group – but after that, I lost my way a bit. I probably got in with the wrong crowd, and nicotine and alcohol became far more attractive than schoolwork. Girls also came into the picture for the first time, which was a big distraction. I constantly found myself getting into trouble – one of my lasting memories was of the very whippy canes they used. The tips would snap around your buttocks, leaving you with painful weals on your midriff. This was the '70s, remember, when corporal punishment was very much in.

What I've never been able to work out is whether my going off the rails was standard adolescent rebellion or the result of something momentous that happened around that time. Because when I was 14, my father died of cancer. He was just 41.

Obviously, a parent's death is a huge event in anyone's life, and my dad dying is particularly relevant to this book as it's all about mortality. I remember the funeral at Chobham Church like it was yesterday. It was an incredibly sad occasion, and I found it all extremely hard to take in. I had managed to say goodbye to my father before he died, but I don't recall saying a great deal to him. It would have been difficult at any age, but as a 14-year-old in that era, it was almost impossible. Things were still pretty 'stiff upper-lip' in England, and you weren't supposed to show too much emotion.

I was upset for many weeks after Dad's death, but I don't think I grieved for too long or had grief issues as such. As a teenager, you are quite resilient, and I've never thought that what happened or the way it was handled ruined my life or anything. But it's difficult to be sure how much it affected me because I've only lived the one life. I do wish I'd had some more guidance and that we'd been living in a more open culture. That's one of the reasons why I'm writing this book – to do what I can to make bereavement a little easier for anyone who finds themselves in a similar position.

VERY MUCH ALIVE

Whether it was my father's death or would have happened anyway, I didn't really make the most of what Wellington had to offer after my first year there. This has always been a source of regret for me. I took three A levels – French, German and maths – but messed them up completely. This was exactly what I deserved, but I was very upset about it for a while. I retook two of the A levels but didn't improve my grades much. Still, I managed to get a place at Portsmouth Polytechnic to do a degree in business studies, starting in the autumn of 1979.

The degree at Portsmouth was a four-year 'thin sandwich' course, with three six-month placements. This suited me well because I was more of a doer than a thinker. I did one of the placements at an electronics firm in Bognor Regis, another with Vickers Engineering in Southampton and the third at Planning Research and Systems in Covent Garden. I particularly enjoyed the last one because I was and still am a bit of a party animal!

After graduating, I went to work for a big electronic components manufacturer called STC and ended up in sales, covering the London area for one of the group's firms. I must have done quite well because I was able to buy my first house during this period. But I started to become restless, and in 1985, I took a year out to do some travelling. I had a fantastic, mind-broadening time. I started off by flying to Australia, with stopovers in San Francisco, Hawaii and New Zealand. Then, after a few days in Sydney, I went to work on a huge cattle station in Queensland before moving on to an even bigger one in the Northern Territory. After that, I met up with my friend Diney in Hong Kong, and we travelled together through Thailand, Malaysia, Singapore, Bali and some of the nearby islands then back home via Sri Lanka. This was well before the tourism boom in that part of the world, and I have wonderful memories of the unspoilt places we visited. The trip gave me an appetite for travelling that remains as strong as ever, despite my MND.

When I got back to the UK, I worked for my father's old firm, Waycom, in Bracknell for a while, but it soon became obvious to me that I wasn't cut out for corporate life. I hated the politics, and I was cocky – I had inherited at least some of Dad's entrepreneurial drive and thought I could do everything better myself. So, in 1987, I set up my own company with a couple of friends. It was called Front Line Components, and we distributed and resold electronic systems and components. It wasn't a great business, to be honest, but it got me started. And while I was running it, a German firm called Wieland GmbH, which was one of our principal suppliers, asked me to set up a UK office for them. We reached an agreement that if we raised the roughly £100K required, they would give us exclusive rights in the UK. We came up with the cash and set up in the same small unit near Guildford where Front Line was based. Right from the off, the business flourished. This was to the detriment of

Front Line, which eventually folded, but I was so focused on Weiland that I didn't mind.

This was the turning point for me. Before, I had been somewhat unfocused and directionless. Now I entered a wonderful phase in my life. And the biggest part of it was marrying Jess. I had actually known her since I was 15, and she was just 10, as her older brother Seb was a good friend of my brother Andrew. But, of course, I hadn't paid much attention to her back then, nor vice-versa. Then a few years later, I found myself sitting next to her at my sister's 21st birthday party. She was lovely, chatty and very pretty. It was also obvious that she had a really good head on her, which I found extremely appealing. About a year later, our mutual friend Libby invited us both to a barbeque at her house in Clapham, and that was that, really. We got married in May 1991, shortly after Jess had qualified as a doctor. I didn't realise at the time quite how advantageous it was going to turn out to be to have a medically savvy wife!

Our three children were born in 1993 (David), 1995 (Jo) and 1998 (Rosie). Jess and I have always been very family-centric, and they have enhanced our lives more than I can say. They are truly great kids, and I'm immensely proud of them. They have all found positive, fulfilling directions in life, which gives me great satisfaction.

My extended family is also extremely important to me, and it kept on growing during the 1990s. Each of my siblings now has three children, so I have nine nephews and nieces, plus another nine step ones through my mother's second husband, Richard, a wonderful, thoughtful man who she married back in 1981.

While my family life was blossoming, Wieland was also going from strength to strength, and I had a wonderful mentor called Hanno Krajowsky, who was the parent company's export manager (sadly, he died of cancer in 2016). We got involved in major projects like supplying all the lighting systems for the Petronas Twin Towers in Kuala Lumpur, at the time the tallest building in the world. On the back of that success, we opened up an office in the city to service the property boom that was happening there. My life became a whirl of first-class trips to the USA, Europe and the Far East. We were a young, ambitious team, all in our 20s and 30s, and we worked extremely hard. But goodness, we played hard too! Our customer sales trips to Germany were legendary, as were our Christmas parties and golf days. My lovely PA, Gilli, who is godmother to my daughter Rosie, says we basically partied for 10 years.

But all good things come to an end. After a few years, the German parent company bought out the UK shareholders, and we became a fully owned subsidiary. Then, in the late 1990s, a new German MD came in, and he and I didn't see eye to eye at all. One morning in 2000, I woke up and decided to resign then and there. I left Wieland just before my 40th birthday.

VERY MUCH ALIVE

Depending on your point of view, with three small children to support, this was either a brave or a very foolhardy thing to do, particularly as I had no real idea what I wanted to do next. But everyone was talking about the internet and the world wide web, so I decided to do a web design course in London. I found it absolutely fascinating and knew very quickly that this was the area I wanted to go into. Then a friend introduced me to someone who was interested in selling skincare and cosmetic projects to men and thought that the future lay in doing it via direct channels rather than traditional retail. I agreed. We teamed up, and in late 2000, a company called Mankind was born.

At first, we sold via a mail order catalogue, but then we got a website up and running. We were very early to the e-commerce party – this was still the era of dial-up internet – and this gave us first mover advantage. But the business really started to take off in 2003 when broadband was rolled out. We added a female brand called Beauty Expert to our range and became one of the market leaders in the online cosmetics business. By 2007, we had a staff of around 20. The business continued to thrive, and in 2010, we sold it to the Hut Group.

My next venture was joining forces with my brother Andy in his children's play equipment business. It was called The Outdoor Toy Company and mainly sold trampolines and wooden climbing frames. The firm had suffered badly in the 2008–10 financial crisis, and there were some people in my family who questioned my decision to team up with Andy. But it was something I felt compelled to do, and I'm very glad that I did. The first couple of years were tough, though. We made some dubious product choices – bringing in container loads of toboggans ahead of a period when it didn't snow at all for two years springs to mind! – and couldn't seem to find the 'magic dust' you need for success. But I was able to put some working capital into the business to buy stock (mostly from China, with upfront payments) and keep us moving forward.

Things really started to turn around when we rebranded the company as Capital Play and embarked on our own manufacturing strategy. In 2013, we hit the jackpot, relatively speaking, when we designed and developed the first purpose-built inground trampoline. We'd spotted a gap in the market, and there was huge potential demand. The trampolines were an instant success, not only in the UK (where they had good margins) but also abroad, particularly in Australia and Europe. Capital Play grew year on year, and Andy and I took on more and more staff, developing a great team of loyal, hard-working people. By the start of 2017, the shit may have been rapidly heading towards the fan for me health-wise, but Capital Play was in excellent shape.

What else can I tell you about myself prior to my diagnosis? I was constantly on the go and always looking for the next challenge. I loved sport, both participating in it (particularly tennis, golf and cycling) and watching it. I could be a cavalier risk-taker without much thought for the consequences – in the early '90s, I won a police bravery award for rugby tackling a mugger who had snatched an old lady's handbag near where I was having lunch in the garden of a friend's house in Putney, then sitting on him until the police showed up. I was fun-loving, adored travelling, and I was and remain a big dog person (I think no family can be complete without dogs. They'll be with me until my dying day). My friends, or at least my wife (!), would tell you that I was a helpful guy, always willing to drop everything to come to the aid of anyone who needed anything done. And I was nearly always positive about almost everything.

On the minus side, I never liked being told what to do. I tended to go my own way and do my own thing. This could be described as arrogant and selfish, and it probably was a lot of the time. I should have listened and compromised more. Instead, I tended to do things on impulse, often without regard to what others wanted or needed. And even before I developed MND, which loosens up the emotions (I'll talk about this more later), I should have been a much better communicator. I was never good at expressing emotion and preferred to say nothing rather than entering into a discussion or argument (well, I am a bloke!). I could see the merits of talking difficult things through, but I just wasn't very good at it. Ironically, now that I have to type everything out, I'm better in that department than I used to be. Maybe it's because I'm more confident that people will take in what I have to say because they have to concentrate to read it!

If I had my life again, I'd focus more on education and academic achievement. I didn't make the connection between working hard at school, getting into a good university and obtaining professional qualifications and the rewards these things would have brought me later in life. I was more interested in partying, having fun and travelling. I guess I just lived for the moment. This isn't necessarily a bad thing – a lot of this book is about the importance of doing exactly that, especially when you know your days are numbered – but I do wish I'd been more prudent. That said, I have no regrets in life, and I don't like to look back. You can't change the past, but you can change the future . . .

As it happened, life had worked out very well for me. I'd worked extremely hard in my entrepreneurial career, and as I said before, I've always been lucky. But I'd taken huge risks in setting up businesses like Mankind and Capital Play. It's true I'd had a privileged background, but I've always had to work for every penny I've earned. At times, it's not been easy at all for my family, and it's only the stability of Jess's job that has enabled us to keep food on the table. The life of an entrepreneur has many ups and downs. In the end, I'd made a success of most of my ventures, but things could have been very different.

So that was me on the eve of my world being turned completely upside down. Conventional but with a bit of a rebellious streak. Not much of a worrier and not particularly 'deep'. Active, happy-go-lucky and very family minded. If I'd been a religious man, I would have described myself as blessed.

Father and Mother's Wedding in 1956

My Dad

Jess and I on Wedding Day 1991

Our first born David, 1993

David, Jo and Rosie in 2000

My three children and nine nieces and nephews, 2013

Updown House, our iconic family home where I grew up. My lovely step-father Richard and my mum are on the left

2

DIAGNOSIS

'Death can come at any age, but the pride of life fools a person into thinking that day is far away.'
John Buttrick, *Fighting Temptation*

The first time I sensed something wasn't right was in the autumn of 2016. I'd had a few drinks with some mates in Guildford, and while I was being driven back home, I realised I was slurring my speech quite badly. This is odd, I thought. I haven't had that much to drink, and normally, I hold it pretty well. I didn't think any more about it after that, but looking back, that's where the story really began.

Jess had her first inkling that something was awry around that time when she heard me coughing after breakfast. Then, at Christmas, she noticed me slurring my words. She didn't just roll her eyes and think, There goes Paul, drunk again. Instead, her medical antennae started twitching. They twitched even more when I told her, on Mother's Day in March, that I was noticing a build-up of saliva in my mouth.

VERY MUCH ALIVE

After that, I went to see a consultant called Graham Warner at the Royal Surrey County Hospital in Guildford. He put me through all kinds of tests. I had an MRI scan, an EMG (which measures muscle response, or to put it more technically, electrical activity when a nerve attempts to stimulate a muscle), a fluoroscopy (an imaging technique that gathers real-time moving images) of my throat area as I swallowed, several blood tests and many more investigations of one kind or another. I was in and out of hospital almost every week.

Mr Warner did mention early on that Motor Neurone Disease was the worst-case scenario, but there is no single test for the disease. It's a case of diagnosis by exclusion. I didn't really know what MND was, or even that it was terminal, just that it wasn't good. But I managed to push the thought of it to the back of my mind. In fact, I didn't dwell much at all on what might be wrong with me. I just got on with my life, which continued to be as fast paced as usual (it was our busy season at work). I was used to being lucky and blithely assumed that this situation would be no exception. It would probably turn out that I had nothing more serious than a virus.

Well, I was wrong. I think Jess pretty much knew for certain what was going on, but she said nothing to me, wisely calculating that it would be better for me to hear it from the consultant. On 12th June, she and I went to see Graham Warner. By this stage, he had reviewed all the tests to exclude any other diagnosis. He simply said, in a very factual manner, 'Paul, you have MND.'

I immediately started crying. Jess was there to comfort me in her usual calm and practical way, but the news hit me hard. My first question was, 'How long do I have?' Graham Warner replied that the average life expectancy was two years. We talked about drugs and palliative care that might help, but he didn't sugar the pill. He basically told me that there was no cure, and I was entering the death zone.

'What can I do to live longer?' I asked him.

At that point, he gave me some advice that really helped me and has stayed with me ever since. I'd say it's a major reason why I'm still alive and kicking almost five years on.

'Have a purpose,' he said. 'Find a meaning in life. Embrace the important things, like the love of your family.'

Of all the things I write in this book, this may be the most important.

*

I leave the hospital in a state of shock, my mind in a whirl. 'Why me?' I rage at the universe. 'What have I done to deserve this?' Then I go into denial. Can this really be me? I just don't believe it, somehow. Apart from a bit of excess saliva and slightly slurred speech, I am incredibly fit and healthy. I have no pain at all. Have they actually got this right? I'm totally confused.

On the way home – Jess is driving, thank goodness – the direction of my thoughts shifts again and again. First,

VERY MUCH ALIVE

there's despair. My luck has deserted me. My wonderful life is coming to a premature end, and all that working hard to build and plan the future is out of the window now. I think about the horror of having to tell the kids. Then there's a flash of hope. I can get through this! With the support of Jess and the kids, I know I will be strong and find a way to extract some positives from this horrible situation. One thing I'm sure of: it's no good devoting myself to some imagined future anymore. I need to start focusing on the 'now', and quickly.

I frantically google 'MND'. This isn't a great idea, as what I find is not very encouraging. The images of wheelchairs, ventilation equipment and feeding tubes make my blood run cold. But by the time we get home, I've slipped into practical mode. We sit at the kitchen table and plan the next few days. We must tell the children tonight, we decide (luckily, they all live locally). Then tomorrow, my siblings in the morning and Mum in the afternoon.

*

At about 6 p.m. on that fateful Monday, the kids assembled in the kitchen. They knew something was up but had no idea what. I didn't beat around the bush. I told them straight out that I had MND, and my life expectancy was around two years. There were tears, hugs and total disbelief.

Thankfully, the atmosphere soon became positive. 'Dad, you're young and strong and you'll get through this,' they told me. 'We'll fight it together.' We opened a bottle of wine and moved into the gazebo on our patio, where Jess and I explained to them what MND was, how the disease was likely to progress and how our lives were going to be very different now. Then we opened up a few more bottles, turned up the music and had a highly emotional singsong together.

If you'd told me beforehand that I'd have one of the best evenings of my life immediately after telling my children that I had a terrifying terminal illness, I wouldn't have believed you. But that's exactly what happened. We were already a very close family, but that night we bonded in a way we never had before. We came together in a crisis and stopped being so damned English for once. I can't tell you how much strength I derived from that evening. What I'd thought would be a nightmare turned out to be a magical evening with an outpouring of love.

The following morning, I went to see my brother, Andy. I'd told him sometime before that there was a possibility I had MND, but obviously it was a huge shock to him to hear that the worst-case scenario had come true. We hugged, and I cried. Tears have become a common theme in my life, though crying isn't something I used to do very often. What I didn't know then is that one of the side effects of MND is what's called 'emotional lability'. 'Labile' means subject to sudden, rapid change.

How this plays out in practice is that I will start laughing or crying uncontrollably, often in inappropriate situations. There is nothing inappropriate about crying when informing your beloved brother that you have Motor Neurone Disease, of course, but sometimes people can be taken aback by the strength of my reactions. And the lability is getting worse. Anything even slightly emotional can set me off. Something that I find amusing, which often really isn't, can get me in hysterics for several minutes. I can't stop laughing any more than you can make yourself stop having hiccups. The latest development is me laughing and crying at the same time. This can really confuse people and be embarrassing for everyone concerned, not least me.

When I had got that particular bout of crying out of the way, Andy and I went to meet my elder sister, Sally, for a coffee. There was a very tender moment when she was holding my hand and weeping. 'It's so unfair,' she said. 'Why does this always happen to the good people?' After that, I went to break the news to my younger sister, Juliet. Then we all went together to see our lovely mother.

Mum said very little and didn't show much emotion. I think she just couldn't take it all in. She didn't really understand what MND was or how the disease was likely to develop. But I need to say that since that day, she has been one of my closest and most loving supporters. She's constantly asking about cures and giving me hope. I have no doubt now about where I get my positivity from!

*

Once I had told my immediate family, I decided to let everyone else in my life know I had MND as soon as possible.

Why hide or delay? I'm aware that many people with an illness like mine don't want it generally known, but to be honest, I don't quite understand that point of view. Maybe it's something to do with not wanting to make it all too real. Or a desire to avoid people feeling sorry for them – that one I could relate to. I would never put pressure on anyone to 'come out' about a terminal diagnosis if they didn't want to, but for me it was a relief. I made a point of phoning all my close friends to tell them the news. I just felt it was important for me to do this myself before they heard it through the grapevine. When I spoke to them, I was quite unemotional and stuck to the facts. I didn't know what the future held, I told them. I was still in relative shock and confusion, but I wanted to show I was strong and positive. For me, this was just a practical thing to do.

Despite my efforts to tell people in person, the word spread very quickly through my friendship group once the cat was out of the bag. I was inundated with calls and messages. Then, 48 hours after I had received my diagnosis, three of my closest friends from my tennis club turned up at the house out of the blue. David Kirby, Duncan Foster and Simon Heilpern had tennis rackets in their hands and four bottles of my favourite red wine, Châteauneuf-du-Pape. We hugged, but not much was said. I sensed they didn't quite know what to say. Better, then, to say nothing at all.

Actually, most people struggled to know what to say when they met me after I was diagnosed. As we all know, as a society we're not good at talking about death and dying. We tend to bury our heads. But when people did manage to refer to the elephant in the room, I was grateful, even if it was only something very short like, 'I'm sorry about your news.'

Most people took the view that they wouldn't shower me with sympathy. They knew I wouldn't want that. I got a huge number of emails, messages and texts and made sure I responded to all of them. I let everyone know that I was fine and in a good state of mind. Whatever the future might hold, I told them, I was just thankful for what life had given me so far and had no complaints or anger about my diagnosis.

Everyone reacted differently. Nobody dropped me, but some of my friends said nothing at all, while others took the piss. Comments along the lines of, 'Well, you might as well take up smoking again, you've got nothing to lose,' were quite common. I don't hold the indifferent reactions I received against the people in question. I know I would find it difficult if the tables were turned.

Anyway, actions can speak louder than words. We played a few sets of tennis on the court we'd built at our house in 2005, which felt refreshingly normal. Then we sat in the garden gazebo, and I explained MND to them, telling them how the symptoms had started and how the illness was likely to progress. As the wine started to flow, we got onto the subject of my bucket list. As you can imagine, the concept had suddenly become a lot less abstract to me. The first long-held ambition I mentioned was to climb Mount

Kilimanjaro. We agreed a date there and then for the following October, and I came up with the idea of playing tennis at the top of the 5,850 m volcano to raise money for MND research. We also came up with a plan for a Charity Day at our tennis club in September.

That session with the Châteauneuf-du-Pape was the turning point, and I can't thank Duncan, David and Simon enough. Before then, my emotions were all over the place. After that evening, I had a clear idea how I was going to approach my illness. I wasn't going to wallow in self-pity and turn my face to the wall. Instead, I was going to embrace what was happening and live life to the max. I was going to have a wonderful, positive and fulfilling next few years. They say change is as good as a rest, and my diagnosis was certainly a huge change. Could I make it one for the better? Well, I was damned well going to try! The time I had left might not be easy, but it was definitely going to be interesting . . .

3

THE GRIM REAPER

'Death is one of the attributes you were created with; death is part of you. Your life's continual task is to build your death.'
Michel de Montaigne, 16th-century French philosopher

Receiving a terminal diagnosis is like a bereavement in some ways. In both cases, you have to go through a mourning process, which typically has a number of phases. At first, you feel utterly bewildered, but there's so much to do – planning a funeral, for example, or breaking the news to your nearest and dearest – that you don't have much time to ponder the enormity of what has happened to you. It's only later, when the initial rush of activity has subsided, that you are really forced to come to terms with your changed reality.

There are supposedly five 'classic' stages of grief. They're not written in stone, and not everyone goes through them all or experiences them in the same order. It is also possible to get stuck in one or another of them – some people, for instance, never really get beyond the 'anger' phase.

VERY MUCH ALIVE

Nevertheless, they can be a useful checklist, in the sense of things to look out for if you've lost someone close or been told you have a terminal illness. It's interesting to me to see if and how they have applied in my own case.

The first typical stage is denial. This is what I must have been going through when I thought, Surely they've made a mistake here. This can't be me – I'm far too fit and healthy. But I'm a rational, analytic person, and if the tests proved I had MND, I wasn't going to argue. What I did deny was the supposed fact that I was only likely to live two more years on average. Aside from the symptoms in my mouth region, I was so strong, fit and generally healthy that this just didn't feel right. A sixth sense told me that my lucky streak was going to continue, and I'd buck that trend. I'm still here four-and-a-half years later, so it was clearly onto something.

The second phase is anger. I was indeed angry for a short while. I had so much to live for. I desperately wanted to be at my children's weddings and see my grandchildren, and now all this was going to be taken away from me. But the anger didn't last long. I was determined to be strong at all times, not complain, and get on with living rather than dying.

Next comes bargaining. I didn't really go through this phase, at least in the classic form of making deals with God or Fate ('I'll be good and give up X, Y and Z, so long as I'm healed and you take this away from me'). But I did indulge in a lot of 'what if' thinking, much of it connected with guilt. My immediate reaction to my diagnosis was to assume that the MND was due to one of the things I'd done wrong in life. And there was quite a long list! Maybe it was the alcohol (I do way more than the recommended 28 units in a week. Pah, I can do that in a day!). Perhaps it was the result of smoking, the lack of attention I'd paid to a healthy diet or simply having had bad thoughts. Who knew? But I definitely believed for a while that it was something I'd done in my lifetime, or maybe just payback for all the luck I'd had in life. The yin and yang balancing themselves out . . .

With hindsight, I think this phase was all about me trying to regain a sense of control. If my MND was caused by something I'd done or not done in the past, maybe, just maybe, there was something I could do to reverse it. This kind of reaction is perfectly natural when something devastating happens. You often see it in cases of suicide, when the people connected to the tragedy instinctively say, 'There must have been something I could have done to prevent it.' It's less frightening to live in a world where there's theoretically a solution to everything than one in which terrible things can just happen out of the blue. But the fact is, they can. Take MND, for example. There are all sorts of theories, but nobody has a shred of evidence about what ultimately causes the condition. Life is full of random events that can't really be explained. That's just the way it is. You can't overthink or over-analyse it, or rather you can, but it won't do you any good. And that's the position I reached pretty quickly after my diagnosis.

VERY MUCH ALIVE

The fourth classic stage of grief is depression. Thankfully, and perhaps bizarrely, I've only experienced about five minutes that could realistically be put into that category. It happened in May 2021, when I was on a lovely holiday with Jess. She'd gone diving, and while I was alone, negative thoughts started coming into my head. What do I have to look forward to in life? That sort of thing. Luckily, it only lasted a short while, but it did frighten me. What if those thoughts became prolonged or worsened? Fortunately, it hasn't happened – none of those demons have returned.

The final phase, which I would wish everyone in a similar position to come to, is acceptance. It probably took me less than a week to accept my fate. I made myself a promise that I would get on with life, never complain, and treat my condition as just another challenge to try to succeed at. In a strange way, I was excited. They say a change is good as a rest, and I certainly knew my life was going to be very different going forward. Little did I know I was entering one of the most rewarding and enjoyable periods of my whole life.

*

So, there I am, then, in the summer of 2017, having, as far as I can tell, basically accepted the fact that I am going to die, and much sooner than I had planned or expected. But what is actually going through my head? You see, I've never really thought much about death before, except in a jokey way. The closest I've come, at least as an adult, is a few years ago, when a couple of good friends died suddenly of heart attacks. At the time, I did think, "That could have been me," but being an optimist and a fatalist, I didn't dwell on it. The same was true when, around that time, I got slammed into the beach by a freak wave while surfing in the Indian Ocean. I badly dislocated my shoulder, but had it been my head that hit the sand, that would have been curtains. Come to think of it, there was also the dead horse incident. But on all those occasions, I quickly pushed the implications to the back of mind. This time is different. There's no way around the fact that my days are numbered.

OK then, so I'm going to die. But what tools are available to help me prepare for it? And how can I make sure it is as painless as possible, not just for me, but also for my family? I want it to be better than that, in fact. Of course, my death is going to be sad and difficult, but if a way can be found, I want to find the positive in it, just as I have with everything else in my life.

My most significant encounter with death has, of course, been the loss of my father when I was 14. I ask myself what I can learn from that experience. How can I handle my own death so that it's easier for my family to cope with than his was for me?

I grieved for my dad for many years. I loved him deeply and still do. My big frustration is that I never really got to know him well enough. I wish I'd said more to him and spent more time with him before he died. I don't recall any heartfelt conversations or the expression of much emotion.

VERY MUCH ALIVE

I don't think I said a proper goodbye or told him how much I loved him. I don't remember the last hug. These are things I profoundly regret.

I wish he'd left me more to remember him by. I only got nuggets from my mother and their friends. Apart from a few pictures and some cine film, there was no real way for me to have a feeling of connection with him after he'd gone. I wish he'd written more and maybe made some recordings. I wish he had documented his life and really laid out who he was as a person. What motivated him, what inspired him and what his passions were. How he felt about things and what his faults were. I would have loved a final letter, or something similar, passing on words of wisdom or telling me how he felt about me and what he wanted me to achieve in life. I wish he'd left me some mementos to treasure him through. I became determined to do that for those I will be leaving behind.

There is one important positive lesson I did learn from my father's death, though. He prepared in advance, writing a will and taking out a healthy level of life insurance to ensure a better future for my mum, myself and my siblings. I'm going to make absolutely sure I do the same. I want to die happy in the knowledge that all that has been taken care of.

*

Aside from the above, what I found, as I headed into the unknown, was that society had equipped me singularly badly for dealing with what lay ahead. Not me specifically

– in many ways, I was unusually well placed to handle the situation, partly because I had such a close, loving family and had had such a good life so far, and partly because I was lucky enough to have a resilient, optimistic personality – but almost all of us in early 21st-century Britain. I wondered why this was. Death is a journey that all of us have to make in the end, one way or another, yet there were absolutely no road maps. Apart, that is, from the ones offered by the organised religions.

I don't want to knock religion in the slightest – I know it provides comfort and guidance for billions of people – but I'm not religious at all and never have been. It just doesn't sit well with the rational side of my mind. I strongly believe that when you die, that's it. If there does turn out to be an afterlife, that will be a happy bonus, but I can't bring myself to act on the assumption that's what's going to happen.

I did have some exposure to Christianity during my upbringing. My parents took us to church every last Sunday of the month in Chobham where I grew up, followed by Sunday school, and we went to church on Christmas Day. So at least they gave me an opportunity to take the faith. But I can't reconcile in a rational way the idea that any religion is more than just a 'brainwashed' community of people who have come up with a formula that makes them feel included and gives them hope and a direction in life.

That doesn't, however, mean that I want to throw the baby out with the bathwater.

VERY MUCH ALIVE

I like the Christian values and the way many members of the Christian community lead their lives. 'Love thy Neighbour' is a principle I strongly believe in. I've always tried to look for the good in people, not judge them too quickly and not join in general 'bitching' conversations when people are being talked about.

In a similar way, I'm not a Buddhist – I don't believe in reincarnation, which I suppose is one way I could have tried to come to terms with having a terminal illness if I'd been a different kind of person – but I do follow some Buddhist principles, especially the laws of karma. This is the idea that what goes around comes around. Do a good deed and that will somehow, somewhere and sometime be returned to you. That's how I've always tried to live my life, and it's become even more important to me since I learned I had MND.

So, I went into this new phase of my life without any comforting belief that death wasn't actually 'real'. I didn't have a faith that told me it was all OK because I would wake up in heaven or in another body. Neither did I have any obvious non-religious path to follow in terms of dealing with what was to come. I was going to have to make it up as I went along. But I was determined to look the Grim Reaper straight in the eye. I wasn't going to go to pieces in the face of him. Instead, I was going to spend the time I had left living, not dying. I would also, hopefully, be able to apply some of the 'good' aspects of religion to help other people. But first, I had some more selfish itches to scratch.

4

BUCKET LIST ONE: ADVENTURES (PART ONE)

'Nothing quite brings out the zest for life in a person like the thought of their impending death.'
Jhonen Vasquez, *Johnny the Homicidal Maniac: Director's Cut*

For most people, I'd imagine, the idea of a bucket list is more of a game than a realistic action plan. It's fun to draw up a list of all the things you'd like to do before you die, but then normal life gets in the way and you end up doing hardly any of them. They remain a pleasant dream, a sort of carrot on the end of a stick that keeps you going. It's easier to put up with the dull routines of life when you can tell yourself, 'One day . . .' But all too often, that day never comes. Back in the 1950s, when US Air Force pilots were killed in action, their colleagues used to say that they had 'bought the farm'. This was because pilots were always saying, 'One day I'm going to retire and buy that farm I've always dreamed of owning.' Tragically, more of them seemed to die on the job than ever reach that point.

VERY MUCH ALIVE

Well, I decided pretty quickly that I wasn't going to put myself in that position. I didn't want to find myself incapacitated further down the road and wishing I'd done X, Y and Z while I'd still had the chance. One of the biggest unexpected bonuses of my diagnosis has been that it's made me actually do the things on my bucket list. On the day I broke the news to my kids, I told them, 'I want this to be the start of my life, not the end,' which they got immediately.

Doing my bucket list seems to have resonated with the wider world, too, if the press coverage is anything to go by. The Daily Mirror ran a lengthy article entitled, 'Incredible Bucket List of Brave Dad', which was flattering, although, as far as I'm concerned, I haven't been particularly brave, just determined to get as much in as possible while I've still had the time. Meanwhile, The Telegraph ran a piece in which I described in my own words how 'A Terminal Diagnosis Hasn't Stopped Me from Staying Fit', in which I revealed the following, among other things:

Guilty pleasure: Sherry trifle that my mum makes.

Motivation secret: I don't like failure.

Biggest achievement: Having a wonderful, loving family.

What keeps you going? I love life, treat every day as a bonus and stay positive.

Of course, if I was going to embark on my bucket list adventures full throttle, something had to give. So, I decided to take a massive step back from Capital Play. Andy, to his credit, would continue to run the business very well in my absence. Sales would keep climbing, even through the Covid crisis. In fact, they would positively boom, with more parents than ever deciding to buy their children trampolines to make up for them being stuck at home all day. Particularly in the US, we would find ourselves unable to keep up with demand. In August 2020, Andy would negotiate the sale of the business to a Swedish trampoline manufacturer – on very good terms. I told you I was lucky!

Anyway, on to the list! As you read through it, please bear in mind that I'm acutely aware that few people with terminal diagnoses, or without them for that matter, are in positions to fulfil as many of their dreams as me, either physically or financially. Even then, quitting my day job made funding my bucket list hard, but I was determined to find a way. I dipped into all my savings, cashed in my pension and also had a critical illness insurance payout. Every time I went on a trip, I told my kids it was another SKI trip – Spending the Kids Inheritance. This always got a laugh, and I don't think they begrudged it for one moment. They're unusually nice kids!

I'm under no illusion about how incredibly fortunate I've been. I'm not trying to boast or rub salt into wounds. I just want to demonstrate the kind of things that are possible if you manage to maintain a positive attitude. Or at least, the kind of things that have been possible for me. And many of my most memorable and enjoyable bucket list adventures actually cost very little, if anything, affirming the saying that 'the best things in life are free'.

VERY MUCH ALIVE

*

The first real challenge after my diagnosis was a 100-km Gurkha Trail Walk across the South Downs, which I did in late July 2017 with my friends Una Bradley, Tony Mitman and Marcus Greenwood, plus my nephew Jack Olsen. At this stage, my only really noticeable MND symptom was a slight slur in my voice. To be honest, I felt as fit as a fiddle, but still, this was a gruelling endurance event. We started at Petersfield in Hampshire and walked, mostly along the beautiful South Downs Way, to Brighton in East Sussex. The route was anything but flat, and it was extremely hard work, but we had a great support team who met us every 10 km to provide much-needed sustenance and medical attention. We were also joined by many friends and family members who walked 10 or 20 km sections with us during the daylight hours, which helped keep our spirits up.

I was determined to stay strong because I felt I had something to prove both to myself and to others so soon after my diagnosis. But it was tough, both physically and emotionally, especially when it started pouring with rain during the night. When we crossed the finishing line in front of the grandstand at Brighton Racecourse, I felt elated because I had managed to prove my point – indeed, I had struggled less than some of the younger members of the group. But I was also exhausted, emotionally as much as physically. When we posed on the podium with our medals for a trophy photo, I burst into tears. An early example of that MND-related emotional lability, perhaps?

The following month, I took a short break with Jess in St Enodoc, North Cornwall. This gave us our first real chance to take some time planning my new future with MND. We then spent a weekend in Liverpool seeing my brother-in-law John Olsen, who was about to set off as a crew member in the Clipper Round the World Yacht Race. In September, we had a family holiday in Pula, Croatia, staying with our old friends Tony and Libby Mitman and their two children. While we were there, we took in a Dizzy Rascal concert at the town's magnificent Roman amphitheatre. It's the only one with a fully intact circular wall still standing and the largest outside Rome.

Having as many holidays or breaks as possible with my beloved family was high on my bucket list. At the same time, I wanted them to get on with their own lives, so I never pushed the holiday agenda. But I guess because it was the Bank of Mum and Dad paying, I did get to see a lot of my children!

The next big item on my agenda was hosting the Charity Day at the West Surrey Tennis Club to raise funds for the MND Association that I'd planned with my friends over those bottles of Châteauneuf-du-Pape. I had been a member of the club for almost 20 years and had made some of my best friends there. This was when I really got to appreciate the depth of goodwill surrounding me. It was the curtain-raiser for our Mount Kilimanjaro climb the following month, and we received messages of support from many tennis celebrities. Marion Bartoli, the 2013 Wimbledon Champion, said, 'Best of luck in climbing Mt Kilimanjaro & for your quest to play tennis at the top . . . this is truly inspiring. My heart will be next to you & I'm sure you'll come back stronger from this experience'. Heather Watson, the number-one British woman player at the time, wrote, 'All the best. Looking forward to following your amazing adventure and sending lots of love and support'. I also received equally lovely messages from former British number one and TV presenter Annabel Croft and Anne Keothavong, the captain of the British Federation Cup team.

My brother-in-law Jules, a talented artist and graphic designer, had designed a T-shirt worn by all the players on the day. It featured a Mount Kilimanjaro emblem/logo on the front and the words that were to become my life motto on the back: 'One Life, Live It'. Jules had wanted to include an inspirational phrase that meant something to me, and for a long while, this was going to be 'YOLO' ('You Only Live Once'). This was something I often used to say, probably as a pretext to go on some adventure or holiday, or maybe just as an excuse to have another drink! Just as the T-shirts were going to print, I found myself driving down the M3 behind a Land Rover and saw a sticker on the back which read, 'One Life. Live It'. This was a tagline the off-road Land Rover Defenders were using at the time, and I thought it was much more descriptive and punchier than YOLO. So, I put the call into Jules, and we changed it at the 11th hour.

The event was a massive success – some described it as the best day ever at the West Surrey Tennis Club. I made a speech at the end, including the prophetic line, 'My MND diagnosis does not mark the end of my life, just the beginning of a new one, a new adventure and a new challenge, which I greatly look forward to.' This has all turned out to be true. In the meantime, we'd raised over £15,000 from the entry fees, auction and raffle that so many people had generously donated to.

Next up was a 110-mile cycle around Lake Geneva with seven friends. The route was mainly flat, so this wasn't a huge challenge in itself, but it was lovely to see the picturesque lake that borders Switzerland and France and the beautiful countryside and quaint villages. It was also good training for the impending Kilimanjaro climb. We started and finished in Montreux on the Swiss side, famous for its jazz festival.

There is no rest for the wicked (!), and as soon as I got back from Switzerland, we spent a few days in Polzeath in Cornwall, surfing, walking, swimming and enjoying the great Cornish hospitality. Then, in October, came the big one: the ascent of Mount Kilimanjaro, Africa's highest mountain.

To help raise money for MND research, I'd come up with an interesting twist, which was to play tennis at the 5,850-metre summit, thereby setting a new altitude record

VERY MUCH ALIVE

for the sport. I'd heard about a group playing cricket up there and thought, Why not? This dimension of the trip really captured the public's imagination. Andy Murray sent his best wishes, together with a photo of him wearing a Kili T-shirt, and the host of the breakfast show on our local radio station called in every morning to check on our progress.

There were 11 of us on the trip – me, Jess, David and Jo, plus seven other wonderful friends. It was a tough, six-day climb to the summit – long, strenuous days followed by cramped nights in small tents – but we were all still going on the fifth night when we made the final ascent up the very steep crater side of the extinct volcano. But it was slow going, with the altitude and fatigue really taking their toll. We'd only had about an hour's sleep, which didn't help, and it was so cold that I had to abandon my walking poles and keep my hands stuffed in my pockets. I deeply regretted not spending more on a decent pair of gloves.

Generally speaking, it's not lack of fitness that prevents people getting to the top but altitude sickness. All 11 of us made it to Gilman's Point on the crater rim at around 6 a.m., where we witnessed a sunrise so spectacular that none of us will ever forget it. After that, two of the group had to beat a hasty retreat due to altitude sickness. But the rest of us hung in there for the final two-hour climb to Uhuru peak, the 5,580 m summit. It was touch and go, though.

By this stage, I was thoroughly exhausted, and when Jess asked me about the plan to play tennis at the top, I said,

'No way!' I just wanted to get up there and down again as quickly as possible. Every step was a monumental effort. But as we neared the top, we saw the porters and guides putting up the tennis net and marking out the court. At this point, we didn't feel like we had any option, so we went ahead and played tennis on the summit of Mount Kilimanjaro, the highest point in Africa. We had achieved our mission and raised around £80,000 for MND. Our initial target had been £10,000, but we'd passed that within a week. The donations kept rolling in, and I was amazed and humbled by people's generosity.

While we were in Tanzania, we visited two children's institutions to offer what we could in the way of assistance. Before the Kilimanjaro climb, we went to Miwaleni Primary School, a very poor government school in the remote north of the country, to donate solar lights bulbs, books and sports equipment. My youngest daughter, Rosie, had collected books and much of the equipment, and we were given a warm and very touching welcome. At the end, the headmaster, Charles Shio, asked us if we could help raise the $35,000 needed to build an assembly/dining hall for the children. I promised that I would do my best when we returned to the UK and was determined to make sure these weren't empty words. After the Kili climb, we flew to the capital, Dar Es Salaam, to visit a very poor and rundown orphanage called House of Blue Hope. We ended up sponsoring two girls there called Domina and Irene.

VERY MUCH ALIVE

As we were in Africa already, it made sense to fly down to Cape Town to spend a few days with my sister Juliet, who was there to welcome husband John back on terra firma after completing the first two legs of the Clipper Challenge. We climbed Table Mountain, which wasn't quite Mount Kilimanjaro, but it was still a strenuous three-hour ascent.

In November, I got my first tattoo. The somewhat surprising instigator of this plan was my 83-year-old mother! A few months earlier, she had said to me, 'Why don't you get a tattoo of One Life, Live It?' I had explained to her that tattoos weren't my thing, so thanks for the idea, but no thanks, but she wasn't giving up that easily. After we got back from Africa, she said to me, 'If I get a tattoo, will you get one too?' I thought she'd been on the sherry! Anyway, I said, 'Fine, Mum, you organise it, and I'll come with you,' secure in the knowledge that this would go no further.

A few days later, she called me to say she'd found a tattoo parlour in Sandhurst, near Camberley, and had made an appointment for us to get our designs done there. By now, slightly warming to the idea, and consistent with my philosophy of saying yes to everything, I agreed. So, my daughter Rosie, my mother, Shirley, and I all had similar tattoos done, incorporating the infinity symbol depicting eternity. This was the first time the tattoo artist had inked three generations at one time, so it was a big day for him too. Luckily, Mum didn't let on that she was on Warfarin, which is a blood thinner, so you're not technically allowed to get a tattoo done while you're taking it. Go Mum! Now you know where I get my spirit of adventure and 'sod the rules' attitude from . . .

Towards the end of November, I flew to Hurghada in Egypt to join Jess, who was on a diving holiday. I was there to play some golf! That theme continued as soon as I got back to the UK. When I landed, I didn't go home. I stayed at the Gatwick Hilton and took an early flight up to Edinburgh the following morning. From there, I made my way to St Andrews, the 'home of golf'. The sport has been played there for more than 600 years, and there's no way a bucket list of mine could have omitted a round or two up there!

I had been invited to St Andrews by Charles Richardson, who is a member, and I met up with him and our friends John Scott and Rich Crawford on the Jubilee Course. My golf was mediocre, but it didn't matter to me. I just loved being there. November isn't the best month for golf in Scotland, and the whole town was eerily quiet, but that just added to the atmosphere. We had dinner in the clubhouse, then walked back down the 18th hole over the Swilkan Bridge for a few pints in the Jigger Inn, probably the most famous 19th hole in golf.

The following day, we played on the iconic Old Course, arguably the best and certainly the most famous 18 holes on the planet. Again, my golf was not at its best, but I did manage a memorable par on the treacherous 17th, the Road Hole. (Any readers who are allergic to the sport are just going to have to bear with me for the rest of this paragraph because if this book is going to be my obituary, I want this to be in it!) It was pretty ugly though. I hooked my drive wildly onto a completely different fairway but got back into play with a 7 iron. Then I thought I'd be clever and take an 8 iron straight over the front bunker onto the very narrow green, which is guarded at the back by a road. I thinned my shot off the toe of the club, and it went along the ground at great speed, but as luck would have it, it had the perfect pace to catch the slope at the back of the green and curl back towards the pin. The ball came to a rest four feet from the flag, and I sunk my putt for a par on one of the hardest holes on the course. I was happy, but then I usually am!

Just before Christmas, we headed off to Antigua for a family holiday. This beautiful Caribbean island has subsequently become a favourite destination for us, and we continue to go there regularly. They say there are 365 beaches on Antigua, one for every day of the year. I'm working on it!

After Christmas, the entire extended clan (my brother, sisters and most of the next generation down) went skiing in St Anton, Austria. It was a fantastic family holiday with a great deal of high-spirited behaviour – I think that's the polite way to put it! On New Year's Eve, my niece and god-daughter Natalie announced her engagement to her boyfriend, Gordon. That was a night to remember, but not for Gordon, who recalls nothing about it.

I don't want to overburden you with accounts of wonderful holidays, but we had another couple in early 2018, the first in Thailand and the second in Moraira, Spain. Then I headed off for a few days of late-season skiing with my sister Sally in Morzine, France. For me, skiing has it all: the lovely mountain air, the exercise and the good life in the form of après ski food and drink.

Immediately afterwards, Jess and I headed back to Tanzania to visit Miwaleni school again. We were delighted to be able to tell them that we thought we had found a way to come up with the funds to build the dining hall. My former prep school, Hall Grove, in Bagshot, had agreed to hold an African-themed day and charity dinner to raise the money for the project. But there were many loose ends to tie up, not least ensuring that all the money would be used for its intended purpose without too many 'commissions' being paid.

In April, I really cranked up my bucket list schedule. It started with an MND fundraiser day at Sunningdale Heath Golf Club, organised by my mother-in-law, Wendy. I won the longest drive competition, which was both satisfying and ironic, given that MND is a muscle-wasting disease. Again, maybe I was out to prove something.

I should probably say more about the progression of my illness at this point because you may be finding it a bit baffling to be reading about my doing all this Action Man stuff almost a year into a disease that was statistically likely to finish me off within two or three. There are two classic presentations of Motor Neurone Disease. By far the most common is limb-onset MND, where the first areas affected are the limbs, particularly the lower ones. If this had been true in my case, I wouldn't have been able to climb Kilimanjaro or whack a golf ball 200 yards. But I had what is known as bulbar-onset MND, which occurs in roughly 25% of cases. This affects the mouth region first, causing deterioration of speech, swallowing and saliva management (I do a fair amount of dribbling), plus the emotional lability I talked about earlier. The muscle wastage and loss of limb control come later.

So, for quite a long time, I was able to cycle, ski, climb mountains and play tennis and golf just as well (or as badly) as before. But I did find my enjoyment of sport gradually diminishing during this period. The problem was communication. For me, sport is to a large extent about banter, idle conversations and getting to know people better. With my ability to speak becoming more and more compromised, these things were becoming progressively harder, particularly when meeting people for the first time. There was also another factor at work. I knew my time would be up relatively soon, so what was the point of trying to get my golf handicap down or working to improve my second serve? Still, I had plenty more sporting activities and endurance events to tick off my bucket list before such things became prohibitively difficult, and I continued to enjoy the social aspects of sport. It was just that the banter didn't flow quite as easily as before.

What I found was that other things started becoming more important to me, especially human relationships. Throughout my illness, I have been continually overwhelmed by the support, love and affection I have received from so many people.

*

The next item on the list after the fundraiser at Sunningdale Heath was a dog-walking holiday in the Cotswolds. As I said before, I've always liked animals, especially dogs. We took our two Border Collie/Labrador crosses with us, and they had a wonderful time. They are a mother and daughter pair called Lola and Hippo. You may think Hippo is a strange name for a dog, and you'd be right. The reason we called her that is that she looked exactly like a hippopotamus when she was born. Now, of course, she is long-legged and lanky and looks nothing like one, but the name stuck. We always have a bit of explaining to do about that one!

After that, I flew to Spain for my annual boys' golf weekend in Estepona – the standard of golf was not high, but everything else was excellent. Then I had a lovely long weekend in Amsterdam with my mother, visiting the Keukenhof Tulip Garden. Jess and Rosie came along too, but they were more interested in the art galleries than the flowers.

VERY MUCH ALIVE

The final trip in April was a truly fantastic long weekend in St Petersburg, which coincided with my birthday. We were hosted by our great friends Jules and Alexei Fomin, who live opposite us in Surrey in a great party house called Pushkin Place. Many a hazy evening has been spent there, often in the company of our other neighbours, Tim and Sarah Savill, who joined us for the Russia trip (on one occasion at Pushkin Place, I ended up lying naked in the sauna, after one vodka too many, while Alexei thrashed me with eucalyptus branches. This is a Russian tradition, apparently, and who was I to argue?). Alexei grew up in St Petersburg, and he and Jules, or Juleski as I call her, had created a magnificent 16-page itinerary for us, taking in the Mariinsky Palace, the Hermitage Museum, Peter the Great's first house, the opulent Winter Palace and much more besides. We had a very special weekend. But we were seriously alarmed on the final night when we saw tanks and hundreds of Russian troops heading for the city centre. We thought we had got caught up in a coup! In fact, it was just a practice for a military parade the following day, and the troops were very friendly and engaging. If you want something a bit different from your average European city break, I can't recommend St Petersburg highly enough. Sadly, visiting this beautiful city doesn't look likely to be possible for the foreseeable future, owing to the tragic war in Ukraine.

*

VERY MUCH ALIVE

As if to illustrate what I said earlier about it taking quite a long time for the MND to affect my legs, in May, I did my first Tough Mudder in Henley-on-Thames. It involved a ridiculously muddy and arduous obstacle course, and I felt beforehand that I might not enjoy it. In fact, I absolutely loved it. The physical challenge, the teamwork and the need to overcome problems turned out to be right up my street.

Later in the month, a group of 12 of us went to beautiful Lake Como in Italy for a two-day cycle trip. For Jess and I, this was a gentle warm-up for the London to Brighton Bike Ride in June. We'd done it on our very first date back in 1988 and thought we'd mark the 30th anniversary by doing it again. We were still quite fit from the Como trip, but I was dreading the infamous Ditchling Beacon climb towards the end. In the event, we absolutely smashed it, and I enjoyed the downhill stretch into Brighton no end.

June was also the month when we got to make good on our promise to the Miwaleni Primary School in Tanzania to raise funds to build them a dining hall. The Hall Grove School Africa Day was a huge success and very well supported by donations from generous parents. We raised the money required and knew there were going to be some very happy and grateful African children.

*

One of the items highest on my bucket list was going to see England play in a World Cup Final tournament. Three months after receiving my diagnosis, I'd travelled to Vilnius

VERY MUCH ALIVE

in Lithuania to see the Three Lions beat their hosts 1–0 in a qualifying match for Russia 2018, courtesy of a Harry Kane penalty. After the game, things had got pretty surreal. We – me, David, our friend Simon and his Lithuanian girlfriend, at the time – had found ourselves partying with the victorious England squad in the upmarket Kempinski Hotel after Gareth Southgate had kindly stopped the security guards from kicking us out. Highlights of the evening had included David passing out after one vodka too many, me dancing the can-can with Alex Oxlade-Chamberlain, Dele Alli splashing out £3,000 on a bottle of brandy and the squad presenting me with two signed shirts, one of which I would wear at the top of Kilimanjaro.

In late June, I flew to Kaliningrad with David, my brother, Andy, and his son George to see England face Belgium in the tournament proper. The trip got off to a poor start when the luxury Airbnb apartment we thought we'd booked turned out to be a single room in a Gulag-style apartment block. It had blow-up mattresses you put on the bare floor but not much else. The football wasn't much better – England lost 1–0 – but we had great hospitality tickets secured by my good friend Adam Mason, and I got to tick a lifelong dream off my list.

*

I've always enjoyed a good party, and we are lucky enough to live in a very party-friendly house in the middle of nowhere, or at least a good distance from our nearest neighbours. Back in 2005, we had held an epic event there with a glam rock theme, featuring classic '70s and '80s dance tunes, a live cover band called The Slaves, over-the-top fancy dress and a vast vodka luge (an ice sculpture filled with the stuff) donated by Alexei and Juleski. Some of our friends say to this day that they've never had such a terrible hangover. Anyway, in July 2018, we decided to do it all again. Glam Rock 2 was every bit as wild and wacky as the first edition. We even had The Slaves back again!

*

Later that month, I did another big MND fundraiser, taking part in the 100-mile race at Prudential RideLondon, the 'world's greatest festival of cycling'. The course initially followed the 2012 Olympic route through London, then went south into the Surrey Hills, taking in the three big climbs there (Newlands Corner, Leith Hill and Box Hill) before veering back into London. The weather in July 2018 was glorious for the entire month, with one notable exception – Sunday 29th, the day of the event! It pissed down with rain all day, and we were soaked to the bone. It was also very cold, particularly at the top of Leith Hill, where someone took a great picture of a group of us shivering by our bikes, drinking hot soup to ward off hypothermia. But my team of around 20 all made it to the finishing line at the end of the Mall in front of Buckingham Palace. Then we went into Green Park to celebrate. We'd raised about £30K

VERY MUCH ALIVE

for MND, so the drenching felt well worth it. Once again, I was staggered by the generosity of the donors.

Paul climbed the Matterhorn in the Alps in 2019 (Image: Paul Jameson)

| COVID-19 | NEWS | POLITICS | FOOTBALL | CELEBS | TV | MONEY |

Incredible bucket list of brave dad given 2 years to live as he travels the world

EXCLUSIVE: Paul Jameson has ticked off 50 achievements in just 42 months after he was diagnosed with terminal motor neurone disease

By Matthew Barbour
14:17, 30 Jan 2021 | UPDATED 14:23, 30 Jan 2021

When Paul Jameson was told his days were numbered, he drafted a mega bucket list – and has experienced incredible highs after the ultimate low blow.

Mirror Article

Rosie and Duncan handing out books and stickers at Miwalenia primary school, Tanzania

Top of Mt Kilimanjaro about to play tennis at 5,895 metres

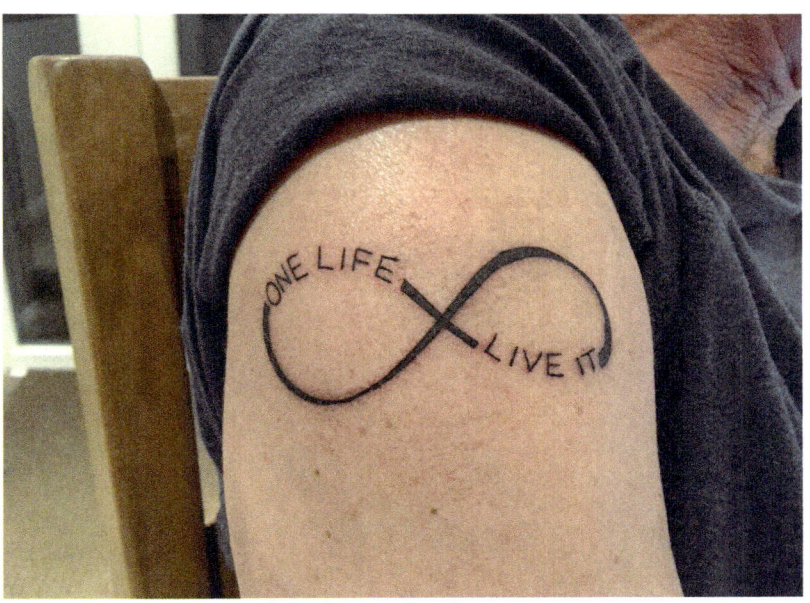

My first and only tattoo

Playing at the West Surrey Tennis Club where I was a member for over 20 years

Impromtu Party England Football Team, Vilnius, Lithuania

5
BUCKET LIST ONE – ADVENTURES (PART TWO)

'It's only when we truly know and understand that we have a limited time on earth – and that we have no way of knowing when our time is up – that we will begin to live each day to the fullest, as if it was the only one we had.'
Elisabeth Kubler-Ross

Earlier in 2018, I'd met a friend of a friend called Mike Sutcliffe. He lives near me, so I can't work out why our paths had never crossed before. Anyway, he turned out to be a man very much after my own heart. An adventurer extraordinaire, he lives life to the full and is constantly taking part in endurance events and sporting challenges. This is the kind of guy who, one weekend, might decide on a whim to take his wife Annie, sons Jack and Will and daughters Sophie and Lucy on a swim across the English Channel (this actually happened!).

When I met Mike, I talked to him about my Kilimanjaro exploits. He then told me about climbing Mont Blanc with his family a few years before. I liked the sound of that. Having been to the top of the highest mountain in Africa, climbing the European equivalent seemed the obvious next step. 'I'd love to do that!' I said. No sooner were the words out of my mouth than Mike was organising the trip.

At the start of August, I went with Jess and Rosie Draper to Morzine, in France, where our old friend Caroline Brampton has a house, to do some walking in preparation for the Mont Blanc climb. We had a lovely weekend enjoying the alpine air, then I got ready for the big one.

Mont Blanc is not a technical climb, but it's quite dangerous in places and requires a high level of fitness. At 4,850 metres, it's not as high as Kilimanjaro, but it's a step up in terms of difficulty. You often need to be roped in for safety, and there's a lot of snow, so crampons are essential. If it hadn't been for my MND, it's fair to say that I would never have tried to tackle it. My family were somewhat apprehensive when they learned of the dangers, and I didn't really have enough experience to attempt the climb, nor had I done sufficient training. But I wasn't going to let minor details like that stop me! I knew I was in excellent hands in the shape of Mike and his son Jack, who some years earlier had become one of the youngest British people to climb Everest. We didn't even feel we needed a guide.

I was caught out when we hired our equipment in Chamonix, though. We each needed a rope, ice axe, harness and crampons. It was the first time I had used any of those things, but I didn't want to reveal my inexperience, so I proudly put on my harness and waited for the instructor to check it fitted correctly. I had put it on back-to-front! The expression on the instructor's face was priceless, as if to say, 'Are you really going to climb Mont Blanc? Best of luck, because you're going to need it.'

The mountain is a three-day climb, with stops at the Solvay and Gouter Huts en route to the summit. On the second day, you have to transverse the Gouloir Crossing, a ravine where rocks continually tumble down towards you. Consequently, you need to try to cross it as quickly as possible, but there are still many fatalities there. It was a hairy moment, but we made it across safely.

The scramble up to the Gouter Hut certainly got the adrenaline going. It involved negotiating some quite steep rock faces, and for the sake of speed, we decided not to be roped in. I loved it! It was a mix of endurance and danger, and you had to have your wits about you.

On the third and final day, we made our push for the top. We were up at 3 a.m. and set off in the dark at 4 a.m. We were well above the snowline and spent the first couple of hours climbing up a steep snow field. For some reason, my energy went ('I don't suppose it could have anything to do with motor neurone disease?' I hear you ask). I was really struggling, having to stop every 20 metres or so, which was slowing the others up. There were a few moments when I doubted I could continue. I asked Jack, 'Does it get much

VERY MUCH ALIVE

harder than this further up?' 'No, Paul. This is as tough as it gets,' he said. He was lying through his teeth, but it kept me going until I got my energy back.

The sunrise as we approached the ridge section with steep drops either side was staggeringly beautiful. In case you're wondering, we were definitely roped in at this stage. At around 9 a.m., we made it to the summit, elated and relieved. There were big man hugs all round, a few photos and then a quick turn-round for the 10-hour descent back into Chamonix.

On the way down, the protocol for the steep ridge section is that you let the ascending climbers stay on the ridge while you move a few feet off it and let them pass. Mike was in front, me in the middle and Jack at the back, all roped together. Suddenly, Mike lost his footing somehow. He fell backward and hurtled off the ridge down the steep snow-covered ravine bank, taking me with him. Before I had time to think, I felt a sharp tug of the rope on my harness, then I was falling too.

Thankfully, we had the experienced Jack behind us. He performed what is called an 'ice axe arrest', jamming his axe into the snow and lying on top of it. His strength held both Mike and I, and once we had regained our composure, we were able to use our own ice axes to slowly climb back up to safety. It could have all been so different. The incident showed me just how quickly and randomly serious accidents can happen.

VERY MUCH ALIVE

Shaken but not stirred, we made it down to Chamonix and had a celebratory beer. It had been a wonderful and memorable climb, and I'd loved every minute of it, bar a second or two! Mike and Jack are two wonderful people with an amazing attitude to life and adventure. Like me, they don't take too much notice of rules and conventions.

*

My bucket list activities during the rest of 2018 were a bit gentler than the Mont Blanc trip. In September, I had a lovely week with the family in Malta, staying near the capital, Valletta. This fascinating Mediterranean island is very underrated, in my opinion. It has an incredibly rich history, having been ruled by a bewildering number of foreign powers over time. The Phoenicians, Greeks, Romans, Arabs, Normans, Spanish, Knights of Saint John, French and Brits have all left their marks, and there are amazing neolithic temples too.

The following month, we went on another dog-walking holiday, this time on the Jurassic Coast in Dorset with our friends Tony and Libby. Then Jess and I moved on to Cornwall, where we stayed with my sister Juliet and her husband, John, in their apartment near Polzeath. John and I got a lot of golf in at St Enodoc, which I consider one of the three best courses I've ever played on. It's a links course set in the sand dunes leading down to the Camel Estuary, with a little chapel in the middle in which the poet John Betjeman is buried.

VERY MUCH ALIVE

The golf theme continued into November, when 12 of us headed off to Puglia in Southern Italy to play a few rounds. Puglia is a relatively little-known province, but it shouldn't be as it has a lot to offer – great food and wine, 'interesting' mafia connections and delightful little stone huts with conical roofs known as trulli. Then it was off to Antigua again, where Jess and I stayed with our friends Ian and Michelle Simpkin, who have a house there. We were really starting to fall in love with the island by this stage.

In December, I went on a four-day boys' trip to Las Vegas, visiting the casinos and . . . I think I'll leave it at that. What happens in Vegas stays in Vegas! Suffice to say, we all had a great time.

The final trip of the year was to Bali, a beautiful Indonesian island with dazzling beaches, temples, volcanoes and much more besides. We stayed in three places: the first was just north of Kuta, the island's party HQ (well, we did have the children with us), then we moved on to the cultural centre of Ubud, where we spent New Year's Eve, and finally we had a few days on a wonderful little island off the coast called Nusa Lembongan. We all got 'Bali belly' at some point, which took some of the shine off the trip, but we managed to climb around the rim of an extinct volcano called Mount Batur and Jess and Rosie went horse-riding.

I have to say, Bali had changed a lot since I'd visited it in 1986, and not for the better. Back then, it had been a quiet, idyllic paradise. Now it was built-up, busy and over-touristed. The most shocking thing was the state of some of the once-pristine beaches. They were covered in washed-up plastic and other pollutants, which vividly brought home to me the problems of plastic waste and the effects it's having on our environment. I made a mental note to try to do my bit to help.

*

Another big sporting item on my bucket list was going to Melbourne to watch the Aussie Open tennis tournament, which takes place in January. Jess and I were already planning to visit our great friends Chris and Jo Guinness in Hong Kong in February 2019, so we decided to combine the two destinations, with stop-offs in various countries between them. We took to calling the trip 'The Big One'. I had an instinct that this might be the last chance for Jess and me to go on an amazing extended journey together, and so it proved.

When we got to Australia, we stayed with some Aussie friends, Richard and Nic Haby, who live in Geelong, about an hour from Melbourne. They entertained us royally, taking us to a vineyard and a road cycling race and much more besides. Then we spent a day at Melbourne Park watching the tennis. It was hot, and I'm referring to the weather rather than the sport! Melbourne is famous for its super-rapid temperature fluctuations. In the morning it was 38 degrees, so we took refuge in an air-conditioned restaurant for lunch. When we left an hour later, the temperature had dropped to around 20 degrees, which felt positively cold.

We then flew to Cairns so Jess could go diving on the Great Barrier Reef. Scuba diving is not for me – it's one of the few sports/activities I have tried and not liked. I just find it too claustrophobic, plus I'm scared of any fish longer than six inches, let alone the sharks that my wife actively seeks out. But each to their own. I'm delighted Jess enjoys it so much, and she had a great time, although she did witness first-hand the bleaching of the coral due to climate change. In fact, much of the inner reef had gone. While she was diving, I played golf, cycled and marvelled at the thousands of giant fruit bats Cairns is home to.

We flew on to Singapore, where we spent a few days sightseeing. This affluent island city-state about one degree north of the equator was a sharp contrast to our next destination, a homestead in a tropical jungle in Sabah, northern Borneo. It was all very basic – we slept in a bamboo hut – and extremely peaceful. No Wi-Fi, no phones, just the sound of running water from the nearby river. We learned all about tribal traditions and practices, like using blowpipes to kill prey with poison darts.

Next, we flew south in search of the Borneo Big Five: pygmy elephants, orangutans, proboscis monkeys, crocodiles and the stunning rhinoceros hornbills. Each morning and afternoon, we'd take boats into remote jungle areas in search of these exotic animals. We were lucky enough to see all of them except the pygmy elephants. The orangutans made a particularly deep impression. They are magnificent creatures: graceful, funny and very human-like, with bulging eyes and long, lanky limbs that make them very appealing. Our time in this remote jungle area was one of the highlights of our whole trip, but we were dismayed by the massive deforestation taking place in Borneo to make way for oil-producing palm trees. It was very distressing to see the habitats that are home to orangutans and other animals being destroyed on this industrial scale.

Our next stop was Vietnam. We started in Hoi An, a magnificent city famed for its lanterns. If you ever visit the country, I would strongly advise you to go there. We did a wonderful cookery course, saw the sights, then embarked on a two-day bike ride over the steep Hoi An pass to Hue with a guide called Lucky. This was the real Vietnam experience. The country is still very unspoiled by tourism, unlike neighbouring Thailand. This was like South East Asia as I remembered it from my travels in the mid-'80s. The Vietnamese are lovely people, and the local cuisine is delicious. We stopped at many roadside shacks, purchasing fantastic meals for just a few dong (the local currency).

Hue is another wonderful city, filled with ancient relics of Vietnam's past, like the incredible Imperial City and the Thien Mu Pagoda. We also visited the military museum, which brought the Vietnam War of the '60s and '70s vividly to life. We were particularly struck by displays connected with Agent Orange, a toxic chemical used to clear trees and plants during the war. The Vietnamese are still fighting for justice for the long-term effects on the health of their people.

Our final day in the city didn't go too well. We were staying in the luxurious Morin Saigon hotel, and while Jess went down to the spa to have her toenails done, I decided to take a shower, which was in the bathtub. For reasons I still don't understand, I slipped, landing full-on against the side of the bath, taking the rail with me and cracking my head on the wash basin.

Did the effects of MND play a part in this accident? I will never know. The one thing I was sure of was that something bad had happened. The sharp pain in my ribs said it all. Strangely, although perhaps it won't seem strange to those who know me well, my first thought was hoping I would still be OK to play golf a few days later at Fanling, the top course in Hong Kong. This was something I had been greatly looking forward to.

I managed to crawl naked on all fours to the phone in the bedroom. I was in a great deal of pain, but I had to get hold of Jess. I dialled reception, and my call was picked up. I should say that my speech had deteriorated a great deal by this stage, but I could still usually make myself understood. That is, when I wasn't in agony and trying to speak to a native Vietnamese. I kept saying words that I hoped would be recognisable, like 'emergency', 'wife', 'salon', 'doctor' and so on. The receptionist clearly thought I'd lost the plot or had been drinking too much ruou, the local rice wine, so he kept putting the phone down. This must have happened five times. I was in a lot of pain and quite distraught, so I thought I'd try another tack. This time, I asked for the manager. Eventually, he came on the line, and I just about got through to him that I needed to speak to Jess, who was in the salon.

I was relieved by this breakthrough, but nothing happened for ages. Twenty minutes later, Jess appeared, very calm and collected. 'Didn't you get the message from the manager?' I asked her. 'Yes,' she told me, 'but he said, "No rush, finish your toenails first."' Aaaargh!

She immediately diagnosed broken ribs and expressed the somewhat worrying hope that they hadn't damaged my lungs. The decision was then whether to go to a Vietnamese hospital for treatment or wait until the following day and fly as planned to Hong Kong, where the hospitals were likely to be far better. Jess was understandably concerned about the possible adverse effects the pressure changes at 30,000 feet might have on my lungs, such as me getting fluid on them. In the end, we opted to fly the next day, which resulted in a sleepless night for me and a very painful taxi ride to the airport. I was wheelchaired onto the plane for the uncomfortable three-hour flight to Hong Kong.

When we got there, we were met by Chis and Jo, our hosts for the stay. I tried to tough it out, but in the end, the pain got too much for me, as anyone who has broken ribs will be able to relate to. So off I went to the Hong Kong Adventist Hospital in the Happy Valley district. An X-ray confirmed four broken ribs and fluid on the lung. Bugger; definitely no golf now. I was in hospital for two nights before I joined up with the rest of the group, which now included our old friends Rosie Draper and Caroline Brampton. All a bit of a drama, but we still thoroughly enjoyed Hong Kong and the hospitality we received.

We delayed our return to the UK for a few days while we waited for clearance from the insurance company that I was fit to fly. They upgraded us to business class, which was a bonus. I don't think Jess took her eyes off me for a second of the 12-hour flight for fear of an adverse reaction to the lung injury.

*

March was rib recovery month. Then in April came the London to Amsterdam cycle trip, organised by my nephew George. Many family members joined us. We started in central London, then went out through Essex and onwards to Harwich, about 60 miles away. We had a support van, which was just as well, as a few of the group were struggling before we'd even got to Holland!

We took an overnight ferry to the Hook of Holland, then had an enchanting ride up the Dutch coastal dunes towards Amsterdam. Certain members of the team were getting more and more excited at the prospect of a visit to the Amsterdam coffee shops! Quite by coincidence, we cycled through a packed park in the city at 4.20 p.m. on 20th April, a date and time of great significance for the cannabis-smoking community. Let me explain. Back in the early '70s, a group of Californian teenagers took to smoking marijuana every day at 4.20 p.m. The ritual spread, and soon 420 became code for the practice. Eventually, 420 was converted into 4/20 for calendar purposes, and an annual day of celebration was born. So, we cycled through the park at the most spliffy moment in the year to a massive cheer and the smell of weed. This got the younger lot even more excited, so they sped towards the coffee shops like a pack of Pavlov's dogs . . . for some well-deserved cups of coffee of course!

Later in April, my son, David, and niece Natalie ran the London Marathon in aid of MND. David desperately wanted to beat the time of 3 hours 57 minutes that I had achieved in 2002 at the age of 42. He was 25, but hadn't done a huge amount of training, so the verdict was out on whether the family record was under threat. David, bless him, smashed it in a time of 3 hours 41, raising a lot of money for the MND Association in the process.

Next up was our annual golf tour, only this time we opted for Marrakesh in Morocco rather than the usual Spain. We had a great time, but it was very hot, 30 degrees plus, which was unusual even for North Africa at that time of year. Afterwards, the others went back to the UK, but I flew, with a night in Casablanca en route, to Estepona in Spain to join

VERY MUCH ALIVE

up with our tennis club tour. We had a fantastic few days, with plenty of tennis but also much laughter. We took to calling ourselves 'The 12 Amigos' in our WhatsApp group, and these warm-hearted, fun-loving people were indeed becoming among my very best friends and supporters. Aside from Jess and me, the dozen was made up of David and Lena Kirby, Mel Redman, Sue Woollard-White (my mixed doubles partner – we never won anything, and both blamed each other), Emily Woodhouse, Jules Thomas, Ian Simpkin, Duncan Foster, Simon Heilpern and Paul Dudley.

*

I'd never been to a full-on music festival before, and this was definitely something on my bucket list. So, in June, four of us (Jess and I plus Tony and Libby Mitman) set off for four days glamping at the Isle of Wight Festival. I loved it! It was one big high, and the music was great, with Biffy Clyro headlining. It was also the first time I'd used my MND disability to my advantage. We were met in the car park by a shuffle buggy, had a tepee in a great location and were given VIP tickets for the whole weekend. I couldn't have been better looked after.

*

Climbing Mont Blanc had given me an appetite for Alpine adventures, and the next peak on my list was the iconic Matterhorn above Zermatt in Switzerland. In July 2019, I decided to do some training in the Pyrenees, where my mother-in-law, Wendy, owns a beautiful, very remote house about an hour west of Perpignan. Jess, Jo and I met up with Jess's brother Bass, his wife, Emma, and their two daughters, Maddy and Josie. Then we set off to climb the 2,785 metre Mount Canigou, whose summit is smack on the border between France and Spain.

This spectacularly beautiful mountain isn't a difficult climb – I'd done it many times before – but it is quite a long one. Six hours the first day, overnight in a refuge, then about eight hours up to the top and back to the house. About five hours into the descent, I tripped and cracked my head on a sharp rock. I was out for the count for about 20 minutes. I remember nothing about it, of course, but I eventually came round with a nasty gash in my head, blood everywhere and a broken walking pole. The team felt there was no option but to call mountain rescue, so an hour later, we heard the sound of a helicopter above. I had pretty much recovered my senses by now and thought this was really exciting – I'd never been in a helicopter before!

I was winched up first, followed by Jess, who was going to accompany me to the hospital. I had a broad grin on my face as I videoed her being hoisted up to the helicopter. I was loving every moment of this! This did not amuse the rescue crew, who had been rushed away from their Sunday lunch to attend to my emergency. C'est la vie!

The impression I formed of the French health service when we got to the hospital was that it was very indifferent and not a patch on the NHS. After making me wait for many hours, they didn't even give me a scan, which was something that Jess felt I should have had and would have had in the UK. But they patched me up well enough. Then, with several stitches in my head, we flew back home. I was due to do the Prudential RideLondon 100-mile cycle again the following weekend, but what with the stitches and my upcoming Matterhorn climb, I thought it wisest to pull out. Unfortunately, this meant letting down my friend Nigel Gibbons, who I had been due to cycle with. I didn't like doing this, but needs must. Sorry, Nigel; I felt bad.

*

After my Pyrenees escapade, I came under a lot of pressure from my family to pull out of my attempt at the Matterhorn. It isn't the easiest climb in the world; in fact, it's ranked as the sixth most dangerous (Everest is 10th). I certainly didn't tell the family that at the time because I was determined to tackle this majestic mountain. It is a near-symmetrical 4,478-metre peak straddling the border between Switzerland and Italy and one of the highest in the Alps. If you've ever eaten a Toblerone bar, you may be interested to learn that the triangular sections are based on the shape of the Matterhorn.

Once again, my partners for the climb were Mike and Jack Sutcliffe, with whom I'd successfully conquered Mont Blanc the year before. We spent the first night in Zermatt, which was strangely full of Chinese people, and met up with our excellent guide, Roman, having sensibly decided that we couldn't do without one on this occasion. Mike and Jack were going to be one team roped together and myself and Roman the other one. My main concern was how I was going to communicate with Roman on the climb. By this point, my speech had deteriorated to the extent that it was very difficult for native English speakers to understand me, let alone foreign nationals. But we worked out some good sign language. I didn't get off to the best of starts, though. When we went to hire our equipment for the climb, I idiotically made the same mistake as 12 months earlier, putting my harness on back to front!

We spent the next night at the Schwarzsee Hotel at 2,600 m. This gave us magnificent views of the Matterhorn, which was starting to look more and more foreboding the closer we got to it. From there, it would be a three-hour climb up to the Hornli Hut, the base camp for the attempt on the summit. It stands at 3,260 m, at the foot of the Matterhorn's north-eastern ridge.

When we got to the Hornli Hut, we walked up to the first big ascent point of the mountain, a vertical climb up to a ridge. It was then I realised that I may have bitten off more than I could chew. This was serious stuff, not for the faint-hearted. I really needed to have had a lot more mountaineering experience and done much more training. Here I was, a 59-year-old with MND, attempting one of the most dangerous climbs in the world. Was I being serious?

VERY MUCH ALIVE

But there was no going back now. At 4 a.m. the next day, we set off in the dark. We had to get to the summit and back in a day, so we needed to move quickly. Roman pushed us hard, and we had few breaks as we scaled the rock face. I had reason to be grateful for the fact that we were roped together. On three occasions I slipped, and only the eagle-eyed attention and experience of Roman kept me attached to the side of the mountain.

As the hours passed, I was getting exhausted and the pace was slowing. Mike and Jack were ahead of me and doing well, but I was struggling. I don't think I've ever had to concentrate so hard to stay safe. Talk about being taken out of my comfort zone. I had to focus all my energy on the task at hand, and my resilience was tested to the max. To make matters worse, I knew the hardest part of the climb was still to come.

When we were 200 vertical metres from the summit, Roman broke the news that we were going too slowly to make it to the top. One unbreakable rule of the mountain is that you have to listen to your guide, and although the remaining distance seemed small, it was still a two-hour climb.

I accepted Roman's decision with a mixture of disappointment and relief. I'd put everything into the climb and could give no more. I was used to being strong and taking pride in my ability to keep up with my team in whatever endeavour I was engaged in, but this time I just hadn't been able to manage it. I was utterly drained, and we still had the more difficult descent to negotiate. Little did I know it at the time, but I can see now that the MND had already started to affect my lower limbs, causing muscle weakness and balance and coordination difficulties. Six months later, there would be unmistakable signs of lower limb malfunction. This was just a foretaste, but the Matterhorn was an awkward place to experience it!

On the descent, we made a series of abseils down the more vertical sections. This involved Roman looping the rope over a rock, then lowering me down at right angles to the cliff face. One loose stone and I would be toast. It was, therefore, with some relief that we made it safely back to the Hornli Hut, then onwards to the Schwarzsee chairlift and back to Zermatt.

Was it selfish of me to attempt this dangerous climb? I knew that my family were very concerned about it, and from that perspective, the answer has to be 'yes'. One thing I can say for sure: I wouldn't have done it if I hadn't had MND. When I got home, my daughter Rosie said to me, 'I don't know whether to hit you or hug you,' so she did both. But from my point of view, I had a terminal illness anyway, so I had nothing to lose. I was immensely proud of having attempted the climb, and it's something I will cherish forever. Mike and Jack have both gone back independently and made it to the top. I'm delighted for them but puzzled about why they've never asked me to accompany them on their subsequent trips!

VERY MUCH ALIVE

*

After I got back from Switzerland, it was time for our annual family tennis tournament, held at our home in Godalming. The whole extended family are involved in this shindig, which is a fun, relaxed event followed by a barbecue. We've been holding the tournament since 2006, the year after we built the court, and it goes by the distinctive name of 'Sod the Planners'.

Why Sod the Planners, you may well ask. The answer is that when we first decided to build the court, we kept being turned down for planning permission. The somewhat spurious reason given was that you could only build a court in your garden curtilage, not on agricultural land. We have no garden, let alone a curtilage, whatever that is supposed to mean. We also have no neighbours anywhere near us – we effectively live in the middle of nowhere – so nobody would even be able to see the court. It didn't make sense and just seemed like petty bureaucracy for the sake of it.

This seems like a good time to let you know about my attitude towards authority, the establishment and rules in general. On the whole, if I see a rule, my first reaction is to want to break it, and if someone tells me to do something, my inclination is to do the exact opposite. I could never work in a corporate environment – I tried it in my 20s, and I hated it – which explains why I've always done my own thing with my entrepreneurial businesses. That's just the way I am. One of my favourite sayings is, 'Rules are made for the obedience of fools and the guidance of wise men'. I believe it is attributed to Sir Douglas Bader, the Second World War pilot who lost both legs in a flying accident. I identify with him a lot, not least because my own legs are now basically kaput.

Thus it was that in 2005, when we'd been turned down on our second appeal, that I thought to myself, Sod the planners; I'm just going to build the court anyway. What's more, I was going to install floodlights to really stick two fingers up to the council because they weren't using their common sense.

When I relayed the story to my brother, Andy, he said, 'Right, let's hold an annual tournament and call it Sod the Planners.' He presented us with a very nice Sod the Planners trophy, which is engraved each year with the names of the winners. We built the court with the floodlights, and guess what: there hasn't been a single complaint from anywhere in the 16 years since. I know publicly outing our little rebellion makes Jess nervous, but – correct me if I'm wrong - I believe we've now passed the 10-year rule, so the council can't do anything about it! The Sod the Planners tournament has become a highlight of the calendar, and this year was no exception.

*

In September, I was back on the golf circuit, travelling to Marbella to play with a group of friends who'd been doing an annual autumn tour together for around 15 years. I didn't know it at the time, but this would turn out to be my last ever golf tour.

The impending Covid pandemic and the onset of MND symptoms in my limbs would put a firm end to my 50 years of playing a sport I have loved and, more importantly, made many friends through.

*

Having ticked a football world cup off my bucket list, it only made sense to go to the rugby equivalent in Japan in October. Jess and I were fortunate to be invited to attend by Chris and Jo Guinness, who we'd visited in Hong Kong the year before. Chris, who is a senior executive at IMG Media, had managed to get tickets for a group of 20 of us to attend four matches over two weekends.

It was a 10-day trip, and I have to admit to being a little apprehensive in advance. I would be meeting a lot of new people, and I was worried that it would be difficult to engage with them as my speech was becoming seriously impaired by then. Japan was also, frankly, not a country that was high up on the list of places I wanted to visit. I envisaged a densely populated country with an alien culture and people I didn't really like. How wrong I was on both counts.

When we met up with the group in Tokyo, they were all super-friendly, and Jess and I immediately felt at ease. We spent the first night in a Beatles tribute karaoke bar in the lively Roppongi district of Tokyo. Much whisky was drunk, and we had a great time, which set the scene for the rest of the trip.

We were scheduled to go to the England v France match at the Yokohama Stadium the following day, but a huge typhoon was due to hit Tokyo, so the game was cancelled. We were also locked down in our hotel and forbidden from going out. But you know my attitude to rules by now. It was shared by Rick Field, who was in our group, and together we ventured out into a deserted Tokyo at the height of the storm. It was an exhilarating if somewhat foolhardy experience as debris was flying everywhere, and trees were being bent double. Sadly, many people lost their lives during the typhoon, and I was grateful not to be among them. But braving the elements in that way did feel like an apt metaphor for the way I was approaching my MND.

By the next day, the storm had abated enough for the Japan v Scotland match to go ahead. It was one of the most emotional games of rugby I've ever seen. A packed Yokohama Stadium saw the hosts win a thrilling match, 28 points to 21. The main group then headed off on a mini tour of Japan by train, while Jess and I opted to fly to a small island south of the mainland called Miyakojima. Jess wanted to do some diving, while I just fancied some R & R and chilled for a few days. We had some of the best food imaginable while we were there and experienced the wonderful Japanese culture at close quarters. We grew very fond of the country, its people and their way of life.

VERY MUCH ALIVE

We then travelled to Oita, at the southern end of Japan, to rendezvous with the rest of the group and watch two quarter-final matches. We saw England thrash the Aussies 40–16 – always a pleasure – then witnessed Wales narrowly beat France 30–29 in an absolute thriller. It was a memorable end to a trip that was right up there with the best.

*

The final big trip of 2019 was a few days in Prague with the family, experiencing the wonderful Christmas markets and exploring this beautiful city. None of us had been there before, and we had a magical time.

The Prague trip effectively marked the end of my two-and-a-half years of adventure, travel, challenges, fun and frivolity. We all know what happened in 2020, but if you're reading this in the distant future, it was an outbreak of a disease called Covid-19. That put paid to foreign travel for the foreseeable future and led to the suspension of many of the kinds of sporting and endurance activities I liked to take part in. For the planet as a whole, the pandemic was obviously a disaster. But if it had to happen, the timing was actually quite good from my point of view because my MND symptoms started to accelerate fairly dramatically that winter, particularly in my lower limbs. By the summer of 2020, many of the things I'd been able to do during the previous three years would have been impossible for me.

I didn't mind too much. I'd ticked off most of my bucket list items, had the time of my life and had never been happier. And I knew that, had it not been for my diagnosis, I would never have done a fraction of what I did in that period. I'd really gone for it and was so utterly pleased that I had. I'd loved every moment, raised more than £150K for MND research and never felt more alive.

Besides, I had plenty of other fish to fry . . .

At the end of the Ride London 100 cycle in aid of MND

On the summit of Mt Blanc

At Aussie Open tennis with Jess having visited Fight MND charity

Climbing back up to ridge having fallen down ravine on Mt Blanc descent

In search of orangutans in Borneo jungle

Jess and I cycling up the Hoi An Pass Vietnam

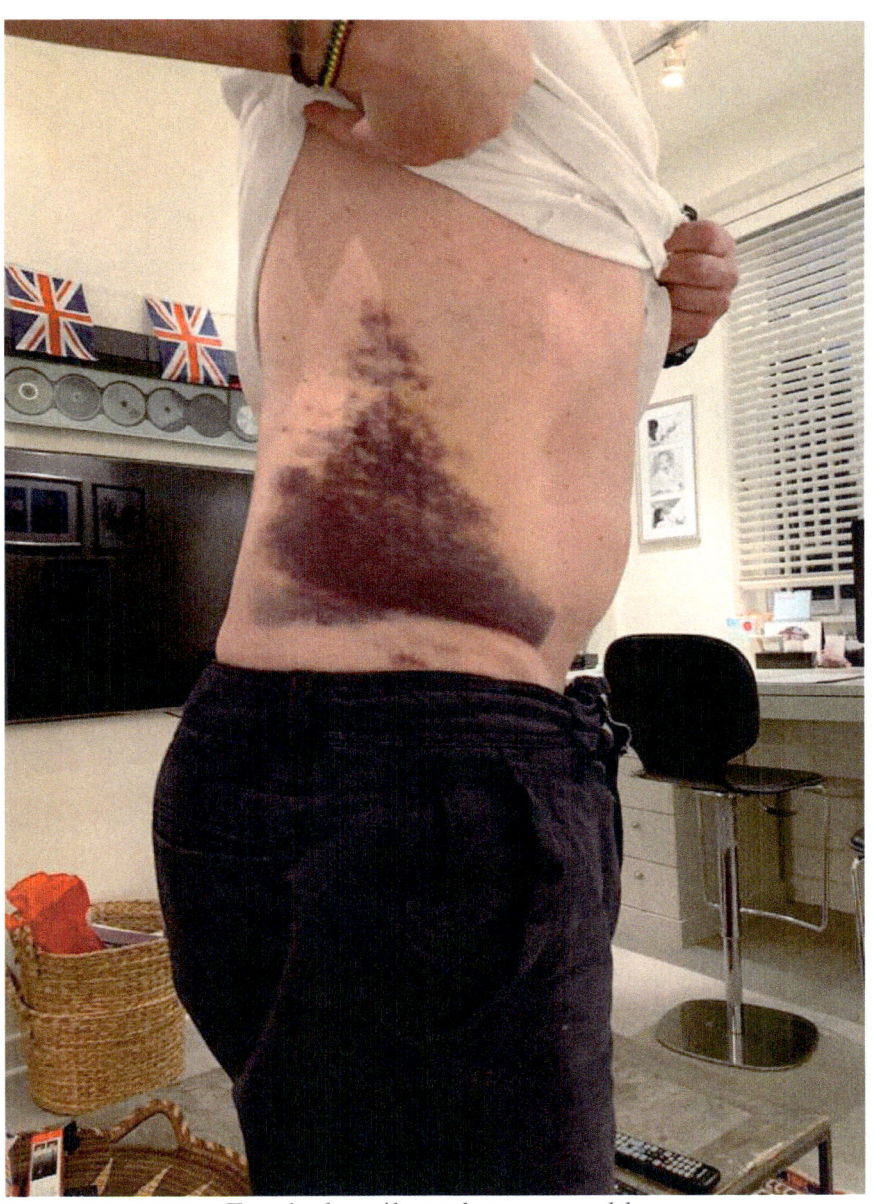

Four broken ribs and a punctured lung

Glam Rock Party with daughters Jo and Rosie

Tough Mudder with David

On golf tour in Marrakesh

Awaiting helicopter rescue on descent of Mt Canigou in the Pyrenees

On the Matterhorn, 200 metres from the summit

Pope Paul at summer fancy dress party

London to Amsterdam cycle

In Tokyo with Jess for the Rugby World Cup

6

PAUL'S ARIA – A STRANGE TALE

'Doesn't everything die at last, and too soon? Tell me, what is it you plan to do with your one wild and precious life?'
Mary Oliver, from The Summer Day

I wouldn't want you to think that completing my bucket list meant the end of my adventures. I've continued to travel and go to sporting events when the Covid situation has allowed, and I'm still doing those things at the time of writing, even if I cut a somewhat unusual figure lurching towards Stamford Bridge or wherever, using hiking poles for balance, or my wheelchair. But perhaps the most surprising and magical thing I've done since 2019 is get involved in the Sound Voice project. I gave you a sneak preview in the Introduction. Now it's time to pick up the story.

When I was first diagnosed with MND, I had a huge support group around me, including a lovely speech and language therapist (SLT) called Amanda Davies. She knew that I wouldn't be able to talk clearly for much longer and would eventually lose the ability altogether. She therefore recommended I 'banked my voice' so I could use it in the future via text-to-speech technology. This meant I wouldn't have to have a standard 'computer voice' with an incongruous American accent.

Amanda put me in touch with the MND SLT specialist Richard Cave, who got me to spend hours recording phrases into a machine so my voice could be recreated. I'm so pleased I did this because I can now no longer speak at all, although I can and still do make hard-to-decipher noises! Actually, though, at this stage, when I'm with other people I tend to communicate via a two-sided flip phone. I type what I want to say onto a keyboard, then the words are displayed in large letters on the phone, which I place on a little stand I built for the purpose so that everyone can see it. I find this system works pretty well, not least because people have to concentrate to read what I'm saying. As a result, they probably take more of it in than they used to when I was waffling on in the old days. In fact, some people say my banter is better now than it was before. Bloody cheek! It can be quite gratifying to find the conversation stopping while everyone pauses to absorb my words of wisdom! But while the phone method usually works a treat, there are exceptions – when my family are in full flow, I can find it hard to get a text in edgeways! I'm also aware that I won't carry on being able to type indefinitely. It's fantastic to know that I will always have my own voice, albeit in a digital format.

Anyway, Richard and I got on well, and we started working together on other projects. One was helping Google develop a new app called 'Euphonia', which aims to turn impaired speech instantly into recognisable speech. I worked hard on this, recording more and more phrases, testing the app and suggesting improvements. Google were very grateful. They kept sending me freebies and even paid me for my efforts.

One day, out of the blue, Richard emailed me to ask whether I wanted to get involved in an ingenious project called Sound Voice, which literally aimed to give people their voices back after they had lost them through illness or surgery. The idea was to bring 'voiceless' people like me together with biomedical researchers and world class musical performers. We would then collaborate to produce innovative works of art.

Sound Voice was the brainchild of the brilliant composer, presenter and artistic director Hannah Conway. She had written operas in 12 languages and was internationally recognised for her pioneering work with diverse communities, but even for her, it was a novelty to get involved with people who couldn't sing! She had a very personal reason for wanting to do this. Her father had tragically developed brain cancer, and this had robbed him of the ability to speak. Having worked in music for more than 20 years, she was deeply struck by how devastating this was both for him and his family. Previously, she had taken people having access to their own voices for granted. Now she wondered what she could do to help others in the same predicament. Sound Voice was the answer she came up with.

My immediate reaction to Richard's request was that this wasn't one for me. I love listening to music, but I am totally not musical. At my prep school, I had been allowed to stand in the second row of the choir on the strict condition that I just mouthed the words! I could never sing to begin with, so I didn't particularly feel that it was an ability I had lost. But as I thought it over, I began to change my mind. Throughout my life, one of my guiding beliefs has been that you should always try to look for reasons to say 'yes' to things rather than making excuses and turning them down. This approach has greatly enriched my life, leading to new experiences, opportunities and friendships. And this had become even more true over the last couple of years, as I'd discovered while doing my bucket list. Now I knew my time left in this world was limited, it felt more important than ever to seize the chances that came my way. So I told Richard that yes, I'd love to get involved. I'm so glad I did because this decision has led to one of the most inspirational, emotional and rewarding experiences of my entire life.

I was introduced to Hannah and started working with her and her talented librettist colleague Hazel Gould. We did several hours of Zoom interviews, focusing on what my voice meant to me and how it felt to be losing it. They asked me all sorts of probing questions, like, 'If your voice was a thing, what thing would that be?' Then they took my answers and transformed them into an aria called, simply, 'Paul'. I expressed concerns about my lack of musical talent, but Hannah told me not to worry, as they would be teaming me up with a professional opera singer, who would be doing most of the 'heavy lifting' when it came to performing the piece. But she must have been a little concerned because she arranged a singing lesson for me in advance of the recording!

When I arrived at the London Coliseum on the big day of the recording, I cried and then laughed at the absurdity of it all. I was about to sing at the home of English National Opera when I had no voice, and even when I'd had one, it had been appalling. The phrase 'out of my comfort zone' doesn't begin to cover it.

I tried my best to explain what an aria is in the Introduction, but Hannah did it much better in an interview she did with BBC Breakfast News, nailing why it was exactly the right musical form for what we were trying to do:

'In opera, an aria is traditionally one character, in a single moment, telling everybody how they feel. What we wanted to do with this piece is have an aria that represents one character, but that character has two different voices. So Paul's story is told with Paul's real voice, but also this imagined version of what his voice could be in its most expressive, powerful form.'

The man who would be providing that 'imagined version' of my voice was Roddy Williams OBE, a world-class baritone

VERY MUCH ALIVE

and former winner of the Royal Philharmonic Society's Singer of the Year Award. As soon as I was introduced to him at the ENO, I felt deeply connected to him. He really got what we were trying to do and was an inspirational guy all round. But he did freak me out a bit by pointing out that the stage at the Coliseum was one of the widest in London!

We spent quite a while rehearsing on this enormous platform, with Hannah accompanying us on the piano and Rakhi Singh on violin. Hannah got me to project my voice into the auditorium as powerfully as I could, and I think she, me and the audience, which consisted of Jess and David, were all equally surprised by how loud a noise I managed to make.

Hannah's final instruction to Roddy was to sing with 'twinkle and gusto'. Then she launched us into the aria, which lasted almost five-and-a-half minutes. The lyrics, which I'm reproducing below, were interspersed with beautiful, highly emotive piano and violin sections from Hanna and Rakhi. Except where indicated otherwise, the words were sung – or in my case sort of sung!

Paul:	I [spoken]
Roddy:	I [spoken]
Paul:	I know [spoken]
Roddy:	I know . . . [spoken]
	I know . . .
Paul:	This is . . .

VERY MUCH ALIVE

Both:	. . . my voice!
Roddy:	This is my voice, and it sounds to me . . .
Paul:	. . . too loud! Too loud!
Roddy:	I was the life and soul! Too slow.
Paul:	Just give me a moment.
Roddy:	I have a life and soul.
	Pour another glass.
	Let's sit together and talk and laugh.
	Let's gather round the table and watch
	the hours pass.
	Shall we open up our hearts, our tender hearts?
	And if you run ahead, I will follow you.
	Follow you along the path.
	Just give me a moment.
	Can you . . .
Both:	. . . hear my voice?
Roddy:	People give up.
	I let it go mostly, mostly.
	I don't blame them.
	Can you hear. . .
Paul:	. . . my voice?
Roddy:	Don't blame them.
	I put up a white flag, have a drink, say nothing.
	But I want to shout:
	'Can you hear my voice?
	Can you hear my voice?'
Paul:	. . . my voice?

VERY MUCH ALIVE

Roddy: Can you hear the softness in my voice?
               Can you hear the laughter?
               Can you hear how much I love you?
               How much I always will?
               Feel the strength of my arms when I hold you.
               Listen carefully, I will whisper.
               Let me sing to you in my dreams.
               Let me sing to you my story.
               I know this is my voice and it sounds to me . . .
Both: . . . like my life and soul!

Phew! I'm in bits writing that now, never mind singing it on the day. It was incredibly cathartic for me. I'd even succeeded in hitting a few right notes for the first time in my life! 'I felt like I had my voice back,' I told the BBC reporter afterwards, dissolving into deep sobs of release. 'It was very emotional, mesmerising. I loved the music. It transported me to somewhere I've never been in my life before.'

A big part of that had been the connection forged between Roddy and me. It felt like he was part of me now. I think he had found the experience pretty moving too. 'It's a very curious relationship to be singing Paul's inner thoughts, as it were, while he's standing right next to me,' he said on the Sound Voice video about the making of the recording. 'I'm kind of used to playing people's thoughts when they're NOT there! But music allows us to say a lot of things, certainly emotionally, that we wouldn't say normally.

VERY MUCH ALIVE

This piece has been a kind of love song to Jess, and I'm aware of her presence behind us as we're rehearsing. I'm singing these lines "Do you know how much I love you, how much I always will?" and I know that's angled back at her as she's in the room too. I find that very powerful.'

'As a professional singer,' he told a Sunday Times journalist who was covering the story, 'how can I even begin to imagine what it's like to lose your voice? I can only marvel at the human capacity to continue positively when something so important has been removed. It's extraordinary how the human spirit can continue with such gusto and inspire other people.' At the same time, Roddy had a great insight into how the piece could help other people understand what voicelessness was like for me. 'There is no better medium than the combination of music and poetry to share a profound experience,' he said. 'Music can unlock this both for the person who's lived it and for the person, like me, who hasn't but is able to gain a small window into what it is like.'

Jess and David had also been profoundly moved by the experience. 'We just felt completely blown away,' Jess told me in front of the BBC cameras. 'We got through quite a lot of tissues. Beautiful, really beautiful. This is something we're going to have forever. When you've lost your voice completely, this is very much you and you're speaking to us.' David, for his part, said, 'Really nice to hear you be able to express the emotions that maybe you wouldn't be able to normally, or not over the last couple of years. We do our best to try to understand what you're going through, but to actually hear it and feel it with that much passion and energy was really amazing.'

Hannah summed up the value of what we'd done in words that apply to the whole Sound Voice project. 'This is about humans, people connecting with each other,' she said. 'It's about telling stories that have enormous meaning and resonance and inviting audiences to just think about our voices that we take for granted every day. Usually, we don't question or think about why we have beautiful, individual-sounding voices and why that's precious.'

I know 'Paul' made everyone who was present on that day think deeply about those things. I hope it continues to do so because we weren't finished with it yet . . .

*

A few months later, I got an email from Hannah saying that she wanted to take 'Paul' and similar pieces of work she'd done with other people with voice loss on tour around the country.

The first venue was at the Festival of New at the Snape theatre in Suffolk in September 2021. I described my live performance of the aria there in the Introduction, but there were many other elements to Sound Voice's contribution. For one thing, there was a filmed version of the project's work, which was played continuously throughout the two-day festival. For that, I'd had to be filmed singing the aria with Roddy once more, this time in a studio in London. It had been a pleasure and a great privilege to see him again, as we had become good friends since meeting at the Coliseum.

The film that Hannah and her team had produced was stunning and very engaging. It was done on three screens in a 3D holographic style, and the effect was amazing. There were three short films in the 25-minute set, which was played every 30 minutes in a small theatre within the Snape complex.

The first film featured a lovely lady called Tanja Bage. In 2020, Tanja was diagnosed with a rare form of cancer growing behind her vocal cords. One week after diagnosis, her voice box was removed. In her piece, she explored her fear that losing her voice might limit her ability to be a 'good' mother, one of the stigmas attached to being a woman with a laryngectomy. Before her voice box was removed, Tanja recorded a video message to her young children so they could remember how her voice had sounded before the operation. This was so emotionally powerful and intense that it immediately reduced me to tears when I first saw it, and writing this paragraph has set me off again.

I followed Tanja with 'Paul'. The third film featured a piece called 'I Left My Voice Behind', written by people who had survived throat cancer but at the cost of life-saving laryngectomies. This too was incredibly moving. Sung by the Shout at Cancer Choir, it began with the line, 'I know I look and sound a different way, but I am still me'. One of the singers was a former builder called Pug Halliday, who says he used to be 'that annoying bloke singing songs loudly and badly.' Now, with the aid of a tubeless mobile 'talkbox' called Electrospit, he was able to sing again with ease.

The main production at Snape on the Saturday evening featured many beautiful pieces of theatre, all to do with loss of voice. It was an exploration of what experiencing it had meant to the individuals concerned and how they had coped. It was a truly inspiring occasion. I met so many interesting people, many of whom were showing remarkable resilience and fortitude in the face of adversity, and I was very humbled.

*

In January 2022, a Sound Voice installation featuring the same three pieces was used to launch Voices Unwrapped, a year of musical events at King's Place in London, celebrating the joy and power of the human voice. Another Sound Voice event is scheduled for the same venue in May. It will feature all six of the operatic movements on the theme of voice loss that Hannah and Hazel have created to date, and once again, I will be taking the stage with Roddy to perform 'Paul'. A couple of days earlier, we'll be doing it live on BBC Radio 3. I'm terrified, but that won't stop me! So now I'm the world's most unlikely opera star, yet another of the surprising and wonderful places my MND has taken me . . .

Singing Paul's Aria with Roddy Williams at the London Coliseum

7

EMOTIONAL BUCKET LIST

'I don't want my life to be defined by what is etched on a tombstone. I want it to be defined by what is etched in the lives and hearts of those I've touched.'
Steve Maraboli, *Life, the Truth, and Being Free*

During the two-and-a-half years when I was going full pelt at my 'physical' bucket list, I didn't really have time to think about my mortality. The knowledge that I had a terminal diagnosis was always there in the background, but most of the time, I managed to push it out of my mind. It was only when I was, say, plunging off a ridge on Mont Blanc or cracking my head open in the Pyrenees that death felt like a live possibility, if you'll pardon the pun. Otherwise, my focus was more on living than dying. I was preoccupied with doing as many physical activities as I could while I still had the chance.

That began to change as we moved into 2020. I had ticked most of the items off my original bucket list, my physical deterioration was gathering pace and then there was the enforced lockdown due to Covid to deal with. So, around that time, I started paying more attention to my inner wants and needs than to external things like travel and adventure. This was how what I call my 'Emotional Bucket List' came into being.

Incidents like the slip on Mont Blanc had made me realise how unprepared I actually was for dying, whatever I might have been telling myself to the contrary. My bucket list had been distracting me from what was right in front of my face. Had this been deliberate? Had I been in denial? Yes and no, I'd say. I had never hidden from the fact that my MND was going to kill me sooner or later, if nothing else got there first. But I think we all go through life believing we're immortal, or at least a long way off having to think about the end of our lives. It's a strange phenomenon, as nobody has ever cheated death, but in that sense, we are all in denial.

Well, it's much harder to continue with that kind of avoidance when you're stuck at home with few distractions. And in any case, I wouldn't have wanted to. I like to think of myself as a realist (who doesn't?), and the reality of what inevitably lay down the road for me was too big to ignore.

I started to think more and more about how I wanted to be remembered and the legacy I wanted to leave for my family. This included messages for my children to read or watch on video after my death. I also wanted to be very clear about what I wanted to happen when I died, especially my funeral arrangements. And generally, to make sure everything was left in good shape on a practical level, including my finances, pensions and insurances.

Naturally, my own experiences of what had happened after people close to me had died played a big part in my thinking. The desire to leave messages for my children, for example, came from remembering how much I'd wished my own father had done that for me. His example was also a major impetus for putting my financial house in order. A few years after his death, my uncle, who was his twin brother, had told me that he'd taken out 10 times as much life insurance as the average person, which was what had enabled my mother to pay death duties, keep the family house and provide me and my siblings with a good education. What a great person to have had the foresight and unselfishness to do that, I thought. Obviously, it would be difficult for a person in my position to take out massive life insurance – you don't get a great deal if you've been diagnosed with MND! – but fortunately, I'd had a decent policy in place before I became ill, and there were plenty of other things I could do to ease the financial and bureaucratic burdens on my family after I'd gone.

Arguably, the biggest lessons from my past, though, involved the nitty-gritty of what you actually do with the body of a person who has died and how you say goodbye to them. My experiences of funerals hadn't been great. You may say, 'Well, obviously not, they're not supposed to be fun,' but it wasn't obvious to me. At my dad's funeral, for example, it had clearly been inevitable that we were all going to be incredibly sad, but looking back on it now, I wondered if it had to have been quite so sombre. Couldn't there have been more of an element of celebration of his life? The next big family funeral I'd attended had been my stepbrother Mark's when I was 40. He'd taken his own life, which was unbearably sad and difficult to deal with, especially for my lovely stepfather, but even under those circumstances, I felt the funeral could have been handled in a way that would have been more helpful to those who had loved him.

Then there were the funerals of the two friends I mentioned before, who'd died of heart attacks in 2015. They were both huge characters who had achieved a lot in their lives, and I didn't feel their funerals, which followed the traditional format, had reflected them as people as well as they would have wanted. The services and subsequent drinks had been somewhat awkward, with everyone not knowing whether to be sad and mournful or more positive and celebratory. It was difficult for the families to know what balance to strike. If only the friends in question had made their wishes known in advance, especially the tones they wanted for their funerals, it would have made everything so much easier for all concerned.

I became determined to make it very clear to my family what kind of send-off I wanted. There was one thing I knew for sure: I didn't want a traditional church funeral with people dressed in black, mournful music and so on. I would never try to lay down the law to anyone about how they should say farewell to their loved ones, but personally, I found that idea deeply unappealing. In fact, the thought of it terrified me, so I started to look into the alternatives.

I've never liked to live by societal norms or be controlled or told what to do, so when I started to think about my funeral, I felt free to think outside the proverbial box. I wanted to let people know that I'd had a wonderful and happy life and felt that should be celebrated. I wanted my ending to be different – whacky, fun-filled, humorous, nothing serious and followed by a heck of a party. I really believed that this approach would help my family grieve and become the final part of my legacy. I think that death, as sad as it is, is taken too seriously. None of the 80 billion people who have ever lived has managed not to die. The odds are not good, so isn't it better to just accept it?

Once I had decided to get the ball rolling in terms of practical arrangements for my end of life, I started where you'd expect anyone with a computer to begin in 2020: with Google. I wanted to find out what resources were available to someone in my position, so I jumped online to see what websites there were to help people do things like write their life stories and leave wishes and information for their families. Having witnessed the internet boom and spent the last 22 years in e-businesses, I was used to everything about everything being available online and expected to find masses of relevant material. In fact, there was virtually nothing. There were a few US sites but no UK ones, and certainly nothing user-friendly and feature-rich.

Naturally, this got my entrepreneurial brain working. Why, I wondered, was there so little out there to help people in a situation that comes to everyone in the end, unless they die suddenly or when they're too young to make plans? A situation that is totally foreseeable?

I came to the conclusion that there were two answers, both reflections of a wider difficulty our culture has with the concept of death. The first was that the funeral industry was archaic and dominated by traditional family businesses and out-of-touch corporates, very set in their ways and slow to change and innovate. Their basic attitude was, 'We do things the way we do because that's the way we've always done them (and, in brackets, because it's very lucrative for us)'. The second reason was that death and dying were things that the younger tech-savvy generation wasn't thinking about or wanting to engage with. I could understand this, having been that way myself prior to my diagnosis, but it struck me as very short-sighted.

It is said that the death industry is the last big industry to be brought online. My researches confirmed this. I saw an opportunity there. Not to make money, but to set up something that could be of genuine benefit to society by helping people to deal with the hardest inevitability of all. An online platform assisting those with terminal conditions to prepare for the ends of their lives, engage with their loved ones and leave enduring legacies. Exactly the things I wanted for myself and my family, in other words.

Gradually, the seeds of what would grow into Aura began to germinate . . .

*

Not long after I had hatched the idea of starting up an online service to help people with terminal diagnoses and their families, someone mentioned Death Cafes to me. 'What the hell is a Death Cafe?' you'll probably be asking yourself, if, like me at that point, you've never heard of such a thing. The short answer is that Death Cafes are not-for-profit get-togethers where people meet to eat cake, drink tea and discuss death. Not, I'll admit, the most enticing prospect on paper, but when I looked into them further, I discovered that they were wonderful.

The first Death Cafe was set up by the Swiss sociologist/anthropologist Bernard Crottez in Neuchatel in 2004, but the idea really went viral when it was picked up by a British web developer called Jon Underwood. He held the first Death Cafe in the UK in 2011 at his house in Hackney. Then he set up deathcafe.com, which has become the 'bible' of the movement. The inverted commas should be regarded as heavy because there's nothing remotely religious about Death Cafes, although religious people are welcome to join them. As the website says, they are offered 'with no intention of leading people to any conclusion, product or course of action'.

VERY MUCH ALIVE

At the last count, more than 13,000 Death Cafes have been held in 81 countries. They aim 'to increase awareness of death to help people make the most of their (finite) lives'. That was an idea I could definitely relate to, so I decided to attend one. It took place in Finsbury Park, London, in January 2020, just pre-Covid.

I was quite apprehensive as I made my way to Blighty Coffee, the small cafe where the event was being held. I was concerned about the difficulty I was now having with speaking and imagined that the gathering would be full of elderly people who were just about to die. Nothing could have been further from the truth. There were people there from all kinds of different backgrounds, ranging in age from 20s to 90s. They were a truly interesting and diverse bunch, and I didn't find it hard to engage and share thoughts with them at all.

There are no fixed agendas or topics at Death Cafes. You just talk. I found the experience extremely liberating. My family have been great throughout my illness and are fully aware of my feelings about my death, but discussing it with them can be difficult because there is so much emotion involved. (Significantly, though, setting up Aura has made it much easier.) In this context, with everyone present being, by definition, open to discussing the elephant in the room, everything flowed naturally. I found it amazingly easy to talk with these 'strangers' about my end of life and how I felt about it. In fact, I'm still in regular contact with many of them. After that evening, I became quite fascinated with Death Cafes and attended several more between January and March, when the pandemic forced them to go online. That was a shame because a computer screen can't fully replicate that person-to-person engagement, and I missed it.

*

In April 2020, I was awarded the British Empire Medal for services to charity as part of the Queen's Birthday Honours list. As the official announcement from the Central Chancery of the Orders of Knighthood at St. James's Palace put it:

THE QUEEN has been graciously pleased, on the occasion of the Celebration of Her Majesty's Birthday, to award the British Empire Medal (Civil Division) to the undermentioned:
Paul David Jameson
Fundraiser, Motor Neurone Disease Association
For services to People with Motor Neurone Disease.

Naturally, I was honoured and humbled by the award, although I saw it more as a testament to the generosity of the many people who had contributed to my fundraising efforts than anything else. But what it did do was crystalise my desire to make more of the time I had left than just ticking items off my bucket list. I wanted to 'do something bigger and better,' as I told The Mirror. So, I started redoubling my efforts to set up what would eventually become Aura.

VERY MUCH ALIVE

At first, I had been somewhat ambivalent about getting involved in such a demanding project. Did I really want the hassle of starting up a new business at my age and in my state of health? Especially given that the usual incentive – the prospect of maybe being able to sell it one day and reap the financial benefit – didn't really apply to someone like me who was already close to reaching his statistical life expectancy. But I remembered what my consultant had said about having a purpose in life being the key to having the best possible outcome with an MND diagnosis, and this was a cause dear to my heart. I decided to go all-in, and when I'm committed to something, I'm really committed.

With all these thoughts whirring around in my head about this new venture and my wishes for my death, I decided to call a family Zoom meeting. I wanted to tell them that I was not scared of dying, reassure them that I still had a great quality of life and outline what I planned to do with my remaining time to give it meaning and purpose.

As ever, it was great to talk, and all my family members were as supportive as I'd come to expect. I talked through my plans for Aura and explained how I wanted to leave a positive legacy for my children. I said that I was writing each of them a personal letter to open once I'd gone and emphasised that I didn't want them to worry in any way, so I was going to sort out all the practicalities regarding my death. It struck me that nobody had suggested this to me once in all the time since my diagnosis.

One of the biggest items on the agenda was describing what I wanted to happen at my funeral, though 'end of life celebration' is a better term for what I had in mind. I had done a lot of research by this stage and reached the conclusion that what I wanted was a 'direct cremation'. Let me explain what this term means and why it was what appealed to me because that says a lot about my attitude to death and what I think is wrong with the traditional funeral industry.

A direct or simple cremation is a low-cost, no-fuss alternative to the established way of doing things. It separates the cremation from the remembrance or celebration of life event. The deceased goes straight to the crematorium and the process is usually carried out without any mourners. That means there's no need to spend money on flowers, limousines, hearses, embalming, officiant's fees or any of the other extras that the funeral industry has somehow convinced us are necessary. It also means that the poor family of the deceased doesn't have to go through a public ceremony before they're emotionally ready.

After the cremation, you either collect the ashes or get them returned to you to keep or scatter as you see fit. I didn't realise until recently that a person's ashes are quite voluminous. They typically come in at three to four kilos, the weight of a newborn baby. That provides scope for scattering them in multiple locations, which is becoming increasingly popular.

VERY MUCH ALIVE

Having your loved one directly cremated leaves you free to have a celebration of their life whenever and wherever you like, perhaps using the money you've saved to give them an extra-special send-off. It also gives you proper time to grieve. I think this is very important because all the traditional funerals I have attended have felt rushed, with the families not in the right emotional state to meet and greet the other mourners. Having a direct cremation allows them to arrange something more personal and meaningful at a later date when they're genuinely ready to do it. This seems to me a much better option than blindly following a procedure and timetable simply because that's what's socially expected. But I do recognise that many people derive comfort from traditional funerals, for religious or other reasons. 'To each, their own' is my attitude. I just think people should feel free to say goodbye to their loved ones in whatever ways they want. I also believe that help and information should be available to them if they want to pursue non-traditional options.

The arguments for a direct cremation seemed even stronger when I looked at the cost of a traditional funeral – more than £4,000 in 2021 and forecast to go up to over £5,000 by 2025, according to the Sun Life Cost of Dying Report of 2021. I didn't want my family to have to incur this expense. I'd far rather the money was spent on a celebration of my life at a later date or given to charity.

For all these reasons, direct cremations are becoming ever more popular, and as soon as I heard about them, I knew this was the way I wanted to go for myself and my family. I even went on to take out a prepaid direct cremation plan (we're aiming to make these available on the Aura website, of course!).

As I see it, the death industry in general and many funeral directors in particular have been stuck in the dark ages for far too long. They know they have a captive audience and that their customers are not in the right emotional state to understand the best options or negotiate prices. The big chains have expensive high street premises, fleets of limousines to run and staff members incentivised to upsell more expensive products. All too often, the result is that the customer doesn't get fair value, while the funeral directors make excessive profits.

The Competition and Markets Authority undertook a review into the funeral industry in 2019. It is slowly cleaning up its act, for instance, by displaying prices in shop windows and on websites, but in my opinion, much of what's on offer still leaves plenty to be desired.

I should qualify that by saying there are some excellent funeral directors and companies out there. I have spoken to many of them. They tend to be the smaller, independent operations, which are modern, forward-thinking and committed to looking after the interests of their customers rather than making profits for their shareholders. Aura has a partnership with one such organisation called Westerleigh. They have some of the best facilities anywhere, good eco policies and a fantastic, progressive management team who are driving forward innovation. But most of all, they put the needs of their customers at the heart of their business. This is why we chose them.

I have detailed my end of life wishes on Aura and shared and discussed them with my family, so they know exactly what I want. This will save a lot of anguish and potential discord when I die. Here are my plans as they currently stand:

PAUL JAMESON'S WISHES

FUNERAL WISHES

What Type of Funeral
No funeral; a Celebration of Life, see below.

Cremation or Burial
No fuss direct cremation, see below.

Type of Coffin
When I die, I would like my body to be put in a funky coffin or casket (which I'll have bought or made beforehand!).

Your Body Before the Funeral
I would like my body to be kept at the house for a few days so other extended family and friends can come and say goodbye if they wish. I want someone to make me up so it looks like I have a happy smile on my face. I want to be dressed in Superdry clothes and a Chelsea scarf.

Funeral Service
No funeral, see below.

Memorial or Celebration of Life
I want a Celebration of Life followed by a party. Ideally, this would be in a marquee in the front field of my house and ideally in the summer months and about a month after I die. I'll do my best to die in the warmer summer months but can't promise this! The formal part of the Celebration of Life should be no longer than 45 minutes (quite long enough to say goodbye). I'd like my life-story images (taken from Aura) to be played on a big screen in the marquee throughout the day.

Songs, Hymns, Eulogies and Readings
Please play these songs: 'Always Look on the Bright Side of Life' (Eric Idle), 'Another One Bites the Dust' (Queen) and 'My Heart Will Go On' (Celine Dion). Ask the congregation to sing along. Only one hymn: 'Jerusalem'. Eulogies from my son and brother and readings by my wife and two daughters. Two of my fav readings attached.

Funeral Theme
Fun, party, celebratory, bright clothes.

After the Funeral
At the end of the 45 minutes, everyone goes outside the marquee and the firework is let off and ashes fall over the land and house where I've had my best memories in my life. Or this could be a drone scattering ashes over the field. After this, beer, wine, live music, DJ and big party.

Charity Donations
At my Celebration of Life service, and also when my death is announced, I'd like donations to be made to the RSPCA.

Commemoration
Please keep the Sod the Planners tennis going each year, and at the end, raise a glass to me!

My Ashes
I would like some of my ashes to be interred next to my father, stepfather, grandmother and grandfather at Woking Crematorium. Symbolically, I want to be next to them; it will give me a sense of reunion, especially to my father.

ADVANCE CARE PLANNING
Last Days' Wishes
I very much want to die at home, not in hospital or a hospice. It would be great to have my immediate family present. I'd like to have piano music (my favourite instrument) being piped out on Spotify and have a lavender fragrance in the room. I sincerely hope still to be at Bunkers Hill Farm where I've had my happiest moments in my life.

*

My family and I have continued to have occasional get-togethers, usually via Zoom, to chat and share feelings, particularly about how my MND is affecting me and how I'm coping. They are all very aware that I do not fear death and am happy and grateful for all the wonderful things life has given me. They are also fully onside with what I'm trying to achieve with Aura to help open up the dialogue around death and dying. On one occasion, we got onto the subject of what type of funeral everyone else wanted apart from me – burial, cremation or something else. I was quite shocked when my youngest, Rosie, said she wanted to be put in a biodegradable urn with a tree planted on top of her. She'd clearly thought about the matter and done some research. I took this as evidence that most of us do think about our mortality and how we want to 'go'. We just don't tend to share our thoughts about these things unless we're given some encouragement.

With Jess and my mother after BEM ceremony

8

THE BIRTH OF AURA

'To the well-organised mind, death is but the next great adventure.'
J.K. Rowling

There was no eureka moment with Aura, no one instant when everything clicked into place. Things just developed organically, and eventually, the business started to gather momentum. But the pace definitely picked up after that Zoom call with my family.

The first thing the new company needed was a name. I settled on Aura for a variety of reasons. First, the word captures the essence of who you are as a person, particularly as far as others are concerned. Your aura is what you possess around you, the vibe you give off; the atmosphere you create when you're around other people. A big part of what I wanted to do was help people establish a legacy for themselves and enable them to maintain a kind of presence after they've gone. Well, a person's aura is definitely something that can survive their death. You don't have to have any particular religious belief to acknowledge that.

VERY MUCH ALIVE

Other reasons for the choice of name were more business and marketing related. Aura is a short and memorable word, and it has connotations of spirituality without being attached to any specific form of it, which makes it likely to appeal to as wide a range of people as possible. It's quite neutral, so it doesn't tie our hands in terms of what we can say or offer on the website. There's nothing about it that is likely to put anyone off because it is incompatible with their beliefs, and little danger of it 'frightening the horses'. At the same time, it sounds progressive and contemporary and works well with the '.life' suffix.

The next step was to raise some money. We took the decision early on to do this via crowdfunding, as we felt Aura was a community-minded business with a mission that would resonate with many people. And so it proved. When we did our initial fundraiser in the summer of 2020, we hit our target within 40 minutes of going live on our chosen crowdfunding platform. That's when we knew we had a viable business proposition on our hands. Up to that point, we'd been hedging our bets a bit in case the idea didn't take off.

Although the fundraiser had been a great success, the money we'd raised was only seed capital. In other words, its purpose was to enable us to develop the website, nail down our offer, and prove the concept as far as we could ahead of a possible second fundraising drive. What we needed to do now was assemble the right team. I'd been in business long enough to know that it's the people who make the difference, and if Aura was to work, we needed the optimum blend of personalities and talents.

The first two people on the list were obvious: my son, David, and his friend Ben May. They had vaguely known each other in their teens through mutual friendship groups and Facebook. A few years later, when they were both 25, David and I had gone on a very boozy family golf weekend at Old Thorns in Liphook and found Ben serving at the bar. He and David had got talking, and Ben had told him that he was setting up an online skincare brand called Skin Woof. David had then pointed out that I had founded Mankind, a brand Ben knew very well, and suggested the two of us meet up for a chat.

When Ben came over to the house to see if I could offer any useful advice, I immediately liked him. He was very personable and mature and clearly had a good entrepreneurial brain on him. So when I came up with the idea for Aura, he was definitely someone I wanted to bounce the idea off. David was too, so the three of us met up at the Pizza Express in Clapham Junction, along with David's cousin Jack. I explained what I had in mind, and the rest, as they say, is history. In the end, Jack decided not to pursue the idea, but David and Ben stayed on, thereby becoming Aura's co-founders.

We created an advisory board and found experts in many fields to help us, including brand, marketing, product, finance and funeral industry experts. In all the many businesses I've been involved in, I don't think I've ever witnessed a group of people with so much passion about what they are doing and such a joined-up sense of purpose. From the outset, everyone has been pulling in the same direction. There is so much goodwill surrounding Aura, so many people working so hard to make the business a success, that any misgivings I had at first about getting involved in such a venture quickly evaporated. I loved it and still do.

At first, David and Ben only worked on Aura on a part-time basis. David had a great, well-paid job at Vice Media, and I encouraged him to stay there until we had reached a point of more certainty with the new company. That happened when we had a second, bigger fundraiser in the summer of 2021. It was a no-brainer to go back to the same crowdfunding platform we'd used before. We had to work somewhat harder this time to reach our target, but we managed it and now have around 800 small investors. They are part of our community and will hopefully become evangelists to help spread our message.

After that, David came on board full-time as our marketing director and Ben as our technical director. It had always been a pipedream of mine to work with my son at some point, but I never really thought it would happen. I'd certainly never have tried to force the issue. As a parent, you rarely get to see close-up how your children perform in their work environment, and I was immediately struck by how very good David was in so many aspects of what's needed to be successful. The same went for Ben. They are both hard-working, personable and astute, with natural entrepreneurial minds.

In two years of working incredibly closely together, sometimes in very stressful situations, the three of us have never exchanged a cross word. It's teamwork at its best. We don't always agree on everything – if we did, it probably wouldn't be healthy – but we're an incredibly tight unit. We're good at respecting each other's points of view and sometimes letting go, even when we're not in full agreement.

It's been a privilege for me to see David and Ben work at close quarters. They have so much passion and energy and are very driven to make a success of Aura – failure is not an option. This makes my life a lot easier. I can leave most things in their capable hands, safe in the knowledge that they're likely to do a far better job than I could.

*

So that's the background to Aura, but what does the company actually do? The easiest way to find out is to visit www.aura.life, but this book isn't intended as clickbait, so I'll give you a brief summary.

The words at the top of the landing page say it all really. Aura exists to 'Celebrate Life and Manage Death'. It connects people with the knowledge, tools and support they need to approach death properly and live fuller lives in the meantime.

VERY MUCH ALIVE

In the 'About' section, we describe Aura as 'a tech for good social enterprise'. The website uses technology in two main ways. First, we offer a range of app-like features that enable those facing 'the final curtain' to make end of life plans and create lasting records of their lives. Second, we provide 'Knowledge' – articles and guides that cover everything from writing a will to supporting yourself and others through the grieving process.

At the time of writing, there are five 'Features' available to members (and it's important to point out that membership is free). 'Practical Information' is like an online filing cabinet or personal organiser, which you can use to let your loved ones know about the practical matters that become crucial when people die, like bank account details, insurance policies and passwords.

'Wishes' puts you in charge of what happens both before and after your death. There are a host of end-of-life options, including advanced care preferences, giving powers of attorney to trusted people and different types of funerals. This feature enables you to set down exactly what you want before the time comes.

The 'Life Story' feature, as its name implies, enables you to create a lasting legacy by leaving a permanent record of your life. It lets you build a visual and descriptive timeline of the things that have mattered most to you and what you want to be remembered for. You, your friends and family are all able to add memories, life events and accomplishments to your story.

'Heartfelt Messages' allows you to feel at peace knowing that nothing crucial has been left unsaid – something I know the value of from direct experience. It facilitates the most important conversations with the most important people. You can even arrange to send messages to others at specific times in the future, such as birthdays and anniversaries.

'Connections' helps you to reach out to loved ones so you can create your Aura profile collaboratively. Managing death and celebrating life is easier with the support of those around you. This feature enables you to create your life story with those you have made memories with, choose trusted persons to receive important information and send messages to the people who mean the most to you.

'All this is all well and good,' you may be thinking, 'but how is Aura ever going to make any money?' You won't be surprised to hear that our investors asked us exactly the same question! The answer is by selling funerals and funeral plans that fit in with our distinctive philosophy.

One of our main aims in setting up Aura was to help modernise the archaic funeral industry. As I mentioned previously, I am a big fan of direct cremation and am arranging one for myself. We want to offer our members the opportunity to make the same choice. This will enable them to replace the traditional, sombre, expensive funeral with a simpler, lower-cost cremation service, to be followed, if they so wish, by a more meaningful celebration of life event at a later date.

Aura offers 'at need' funerals, where arrangements are only made once the person has died, and will soon be offering prepaid funeral plans, once the business is approved by the FCA (Financial Conduct Authority). In either case, our emphasis will be on providing much more support for families than is standard in the industry. As someone with a terminal illness, I have been shocked by the way certain funeral providers treat their customers. At Aura, we want to do things differently.

From the end of July 2022, it will be illegal for any organisation to sell funeral plans in the UK without FCA authorisation. We totally agree with that development – there are far too many unscrupulous organisations out there trying to sell substandard funeral plans to vulnerable people. Aura is in the process of submitting the best possible application. We are more than confident of success because Aura's values are fundamentally aligned with what the FCA is trying to achieve through regulation. Hopefully, by the time you read this, our funeral plan service will be up, running and thriving. We're even thinking of introducing a new word into the English language to describe what we will be offering – not a 'funeral' but a 'celebral'!

*

VERY MUCH ALIVE

The above are the practical aspects of Aura, but equally important is its spirit – its aura, in fact. The section entitled 'Aura Mentality' succinctly captures what we are all about:
- Embracing death to embrace life.
- Seeking to discover death rather than hide from it.
- Being liberated, not shackled by the constraints of time.
- Savouring the people, places and moments we treasure most.
- Living what we have left of our existence to the fullest.

With these principles in mind, we have also set up two Facebook groups: Death Chat, a kind of online death cafe which provides a safe, non-judgemental space for talking about and engaging with the topic of death, and Grief Chat, where bereaved people can share their pain and offer support to others.

As I said in an interview I did with The Mirror, 'Aura's more than just tying up loose ends; it's about positively engaging with impending death. Death should be a celebration of life, not something we avoid discussing like a bad smell. I might only have a few months, or a few years, left. When I'm gone, I want to feel proud of what I've left behind, how I've inspired others to embrace life and also death.'

The amazing feedback we have received has left us in no doubt that what we are doing with Aura is both valuable and important. Here are just three examples:

VERY MUCH ALIVE

'I signed up to the Aura account . . . Holy crap I needed this for Mum so bad! You guys have thought of everything! It's amazing!! I love the attention to detail on it, it's realistic, practical and has an emotional aspect to it too for the memories. Bloody brilliant! One space for everything!'

- Freddie Dicks

'A wonderful, compassionate platform. The one certain thing in life is death, and I've never understood the taboo aspect of it. Talking often removes fear of any subject and this is one subject of which we all have experience, eventually.'

- Eileen Nicholson

'What a great platform. Working as a bereavement counsellor I hear all the time that the grieving process is halted, disrupted and chaotic because important conversations and plans were never had or made, and it often tears families apart at a time when they would normally pull together. Thank you.'

- Phree Brody

I hope this has given you some idea of what Aura can do for other people. But what about me and my family?

On a personal level, Aura has provided me with exactly the kind of purpose my consultant said was so important when he gave me my MND diagnosis. I see many people in my situation do very little except bemoan their lot, and especially during lockdown, I could have been bored out of my mind. Instead, Aura has given my life a huge sense of direction and meaning. It keeps my mind very active and doesn't give me the time to dwell on my wider health issues. It's a business that I desperately want to make a success of, but I realise that nothing is guaranteed. At the same time, 'success is a journey, not a destination', as the old saying goes. In that respect, Aura has already been a massive success.

I've also experienced first-hand the benefits of the things Aura helps others to do. I'm very glad, for example, that I have made my will. I felt little emotion doing it, to be honest – it just felt like a job that had to be done and got out of the way – but I know how much having written it will help my family cometh the hour. And it didn't feel like I was tempting fate, just being responsible.

I've also found writing my life story a rewarding and enriching experience – not the version you're reading now, although that too, of course, but the one on the Aura website. As always, getting started was the hardest thing. Once I got going, I really enjoyed the reminiscing and storytelling, as well as digging out old photos and finding new ones. The whole process was uplifting and reinforced the feeling that I have had a great life. It's a huge relief to know that the details of my time on the planet will not be lost and that I've left a legacy for my children and their children.

Making videos for my family has been similarly rewarding. If you want to remember a life and learn from it, you have to record it. I know I said earlier that I wish my father had left me more to remember him by, but he was an avid cine camera enthusiast, and for many years there were reels and reels of his film gathering dust in my mum's attic. When I was between jobs, I decided to take on the task of sorting the tapes out, digitising them and editing them. It was a huge undertaking, which took me several hundred hours. But I'm so pleased I did it. I now have a huge collection of videos stretching back to my parents' wedding in 1956. This means that I feel I have my own life on film, never mind Dad's. This has helped me, in turn, to make a really comprehensive video record of my life for my family, both current and future, to look back on.

As far as the family as a whole goes, I'd describe Aura's effect as transformative. It has given us a focal point for discussing and coming to terms with what we all know is waiting for me around the corner. Even a family as engaged with the subject of death as we are can find it difficult to bring up the topic, and Aura has assisted us with that immeasurably. I'm sure having talked everything through so thoroughly will help everyone with the grieving process when the time comes. Discussing things openly with family members has brought me peace because I know I've done all I can to help prepare them for what is bound to be a difficult time. Aura can do a lot, but it can't totally eliminate that dimension.

The one thing that upsets me is that I won't be at my own celebration of life party. That thought gives me terrible FOMO! I'm actually thinking of having a pre-death farewell party (often called a Living Funeral) to get around that problem, but that may be too macabre. We'll see . . .

What I can do now, and I think this is extremely important, is line up the right person to preside over the celebration of my life. And because that's exactly what I want my send-off to be, the appropriate job description is 'celebrant'. This is someone who leads the funeral ceremony or its equivalent and looks after the wishes of the family.

Celebrants may sound like a modern phenomenon, but before the development of the funeral industry and the world of funeral directors, they were the first port of call when someone died. I wish this was still the case. Celebrants are often able to offer much more holistic advice and comfort to a family than a commercially minded funeral director could, and they can be a huge emotional support. Some of the most interesting people I've met through Aura have been the celebrants the project has brought me into contact with.

Most people take advice from funeral directors when they choose a celebrant, but many do their own homework and research. I'm in the process of doing this myself. I want someone to give the day some structure and perform a 'maître d'' role, but that person must reflect my personality. They need to not be too serious or sombre, have a sense of humour and at all times convey a sense of positivity. And they need to be prepared to turn anyone who wears a single item of black clothing away at the door!

VERY MUCH ALIVE

The right person will emerge in due course. In the meantime, when I contemplate my death, I feel prepared, organised and at peace with myself. I am sometimes a little sad that I won't be able to continue to experience all the wonderful things life brings, but I totally accept it. After all, all good things have to come to an end eventually . . .

David, Ben and I working on Aura

VERY MUCH ALIVE

9

LOVE, LAUGHTER, GENEROSITY AND KINDNESS

'Unable are the loved to die, for love is immortality.'
Emily Dickinson

Hopefully, by now you will be getting the message that there can be upsides to having a terminal illness. One of the biggest, for me, has been getting my priorities straight. Knowing that I probably don't have much time left has really sorted out the wheat from the chaff. I am now far clearer than I was before about what really matters to me. Four things stand out in particular: love, laughter, generosity and kindness.

Love

Rob Burrow is a former professional rugby league player who was diagnosed with MND in 2019. Sadly, his progression seems to be very quick, but he certainly hasn't been sitting on his hands. He and his supporters, especially his teammate Kevin Sinfield, have raised huge sums of money for MND while greatly increasing the profile and awareness of the disease through the media. He has also written a wonderful book called Too Many Reasons to Live. In it, he says:

'What MND patients want most is to be surrounded by love. Why? Because we know we haven't got as much time as we'd want. But everyone's dying, when you think about it. From the moment you're born, you've only got so long left. So why not surround yourself with love all the time, like I've tried to? Why wait for the rough patch?'

I don't want to indulge in stereotypes, but Rob is a Yorkshireman, so talking openly about things like love probably comes no more naturally to him than to an ex-public school boy brought up in Surrey in the 'stiff upper lip' 1960s and '70s like me. But in my opinion, that makes it even more important to listen to what he's saying. And for me, he's absolutely nailed it. Love is incredibly important to people with MND. Actually, of course, it's incredibly important to everyone, but some of us have needed the nudge of a terminal condition to become fully aware of that fact. As Rob says, why wait until you have one of those? These are great words of wisdom.

Since my diagnosis, I have been surrounded by love and affection from so many people, family, friends and strangers alike. That's one of the main reasons why I've been able to stay so strong.

My relationship with Jess, who I love very much, has grown stronger in the last five years, or perhaps it's just moved into another dimension. This may, of course, have something to do with the fact that we never argue anymore because I have no voice now and can't answer back!

On many levels, Jess and I are opposites. She wears her heart on her sleeve; I bottle my emotions up, or at least I used to until the lability kicked in. She is sensible and law-abiding, while I am distinctly not. She is measured and sensible; I'm gung-ho, with a 'fuck it' attitude to most things. Jess has pursued a well-respected professional medical career, while I've dabbled in business ideas, never quite knowing in what direction I was heading or whether we'd even have bread on the table. Jess is controlled; I'm uncontrollable. She counts the number of alcohol units she consumes each week, whereas I don't dare. She is always right, and I'm always wrong!

I often wonder where I'd be if I hadn't met her. Jess has brought stability to my life. I think on a subconscious level, I knew I needed this, and that was a major part of what attracted me to her in the first place. Heaven knows what attracted her to me!

I'm very proud that we've been successfully married for over 30 years. We have so many things in common: the same strong family values, our love of animals, food, travel, adventure, keeping active and much more besides.

We have also managed to have three wonderful children who we love dearly, and never more than since my diagnosis. Kids, before you get carried away, you are not perfect, far from it – nobody is. But you do seem to have a good mix of Jess and me in you (although I have sometimes wondered!), and that's fun to observe.

MND, then, has had the unexpected side effect of bringing more love into my life. But this hasn't happened in a vacuum. It's been interesting to see how, over the past decade, the traditional stiff upper lip British male persona has been broken down into a more loving and caring version, and I've definitely been a beneficiary of this shift in society. Ten years ago, I'd never have signed off a text or email to a male friend with a kiss. Now I do it the whole time, sometimes even a double kiss with a heart emoji!

Meanwhile, the man hug has become mainstream. It now seems very formal and out of place to shake someone's hand. I've always been a big hugger, but it's become my default way of greeting people, not least because I can no longer do it verbally. This is great – what better way is there to show affection? I also touch people a lot – appropriately, of course! More often than not, I do it to help me with my balance, but the net effect is to strengthen my bonds with the people around me. Many leading neuroscientists agree that touch is vital for our health, happiness and creating a sense of connectedness with others. I fully intend to carry on hugging.

This reading, from 1 Corinthians, Chapter 13 is a popular choice at funerals, particularly the traditional kind that I'm generally pretty ambivalent about. The fact that I'm including it here shows just how wise and powerful I think it is. It captures perfectly what may be the biggest of the many lessons my illness has taught me – that love is the most important thing of all:

If I speak in the tongues of men or of angels, but do not have love, I am only a resounding gong or a clanging cymbal. If I have the gift of prophecy and can fathom all mysteries and all knowledge, and if I have a faith that can move mountains, but do not have love, I am nothing. If I give all I possess to the poor and give over my body to hardship that I may boast, but do not have love, I gain nothing.

Love is patient, love is kind. It does not envy, it does not boast, it is not proud. It does not dishonour others, it is not self-seeking, it is not easily angered, it keeps no record of wrongs. Love does not delight in evil but rejoices with the truth. It always protects, always trusts, always hopes, always perseveres.

VERY MUCH ALIVE

Laughter

I've previously mentioned the emotional lability aspect of MND, which causes me to have bouts of uncontrollable laughing or crying, often at inappropriate times. The positive side to this is that it has given me a good coping mechanism for when something goes wrong – I just laugh it off!

On a recent holiday, I decided to go for a swim in the sea. When I say swim, it was actually more of a 'bob', as I no longer have the muscle strength to do any real swimming. So it was on with a natty blue lifejacket and then a matter of doing my best not to drown.

I went into the sea with Jess holding onto me tightly. The water was quite choppy, and I had to negotiate the waves, trying my best to stay on two feet as I slowly made my way to the edge of a steep ledge under the water. It nearly caught me off guard, but I managed to get beyond it into the open sea, where I had a good bob.

The problems began when I tried to get out. Every time I tried to get back up the ledge, the force of the receding waves knocked me off balance and down I went. A number of onlookers on the beach were worried and volunteered to help. They were somewhat surprised to find me laughing hysterically at the situation. I just saw the funny side of it and couldn't stop myself! Eventually, I was helped out to safety, receiving some very strange looks from people on the beach. They must have been wondering why on earth I found this potentially dangerous situation so hilarious.

On the same holiday, I stood at the side of a pool at the deep end and decided to be brave and jump in. I put my left leg forward and asked my brain to tell my right leg to push me upwards and forward, but the message to my leg muscles completely failed to get through. The result was a glorious belly flop into the pool. Again, all I could do was laugh, to the bemusement of the many onlookers.

Another time, I went to the local garage to fill up with petrol and tripped getting out of the car. I fell heavily, banging my head on the concrete, and wound up wedged between the pumps and a wheel of the car. I was totally stranded with no way to get up. For some reason, I just started laughing at my predicament. Some other customers came over to help me up and simply couldn't fathom why I was howling with laughter. I got some very strange looks indeed. It didn't help that I couldn't explain my condition, owing to my inability to speak. They must have thought I'd come from an alien planet. Once they'd helped me up, they drove off very quickly.

We all know laughter and a sense of humour can be great tonics. They certainly help me when things don't go to plan. I choose to laugh and find the funny side. This is one of the many ways I have learnt to live well with MND.

Carolyn Hornblow, in her excellent book, After a Life-Threatening Diagnosis...What's Next? explains that:

VERY MUCH ALIVE

'Over the last few years, laughter therapy has become a well-established concept. The phrase "Laughter is the best medicine" has been proven to be true. Laughter causes the stomach and abdominal organs to be massaged by the rib cage, abdominal muscles to expand and contract aiding lymph movement. Endorphins are released which make you feel better as they are the natural 'feel good' hormones that we can produce in our bodies. If you laugh till the tears roll down your face, it can be a tremendous release of tension.'

I have many trips and falls. The muscles in my legs are so weak that my foot sometimes doesn't lift when I walk, despite my best intentions. A small impediment can then cause me to stumble, and I don't have the balance and coordination to prevent it. And when I go down, it's a bit like falling over with your hands in your pockets. I don't have the reaction time to put my hands out in the normal self-protective reflex, so it's often my head that makes contact with the ground first.

This happened recently when I walked into a pub on a trip to Wales (note the 'walking in' – I hadn't started drinking yet). I turned down a corridor and totally missed a clear and obvious sign warning customers to 'mind the step'. I also failed to notice the yellow and black tape on the four-inch step and the handrail next to it – where was my mind? The upshot was that I headbutted the tiled floor, resulting in a nasty cut to the forehead, a bloody nose and much loss of pride. But I still managed to come up laughing.

I'm also a great believer in smiling. I can't greet people with words, so I try to put a big smile on my face instead. I find that it's infectious. Rob Burrow is a great example of the positive effects of smiling. I have never seen him not doing it.

I immediately connect better with people who are smiling. Ed, my lovely personal trainer, always greets me at the door with a big grin. We then have training sessions augmented by my two dogs, who jump all over me and lick my face when I'm flat on my back. This invariably sets me off in hysterics. I'm sure the therapeutic benefits of the laughter are at least as beneficial as the stretching and strengthening exercises.

Generosity

When I did my first fundraiser for the Kilimanjaro climb, we had an initial target of £10,000. We reached that figure within a week. We raised it to £50,000 and eventually finished with around £80,000. I was staggered and humbled by everyone's generosity and messages of goodwill. I had never realised before that I knew so many people who cared so much and were willing to dip their hands into their pockets.

The same went for the initial Aura fundraiser in the summer of 2020. Many friends chipped in, and I'm sure that they felt at the time that this was money they'd never see back again. They just invested to support me and a venture I cared passionately about. Fortunately, the business is going from strength to strength. Nothing would make me happier than to handsomely repay the many people who showed so much faith in the Aura concept.

Generosity can also take many forms apart from the financial. Actions that display what you might call generosity of spirit are just as important, and maybe more so.

My friends have been generous in so many ways since they learned I had MND, organising fundraisers, attending fundraising events, supporting my other endeavours and looking for ways to keep me involved in things like sport, which have meant so much to me throughout my life but which I can no longer do.

I mentioned to my tennis friends that, having had to give up the sport, the thing that I feared most was being left out of the scene surrounding it – the social events and so on. Duncan came up with an ingenious solution: if I couldn't come to the club to play tennis, then the club would come to me! Every Wednesday, several of my mates roll up at my house for a tennis session. I greatly enjoy watching them battle it out on court while I drink beer and heckle from the side lines. I'm truly grateful to them for keeping me involved in this way.

I'm regularly invited to events like music festivals, football matches and rugby internationals at Twickenham (debenture tickets – thank you, Marc!). I just say yes to everything! I've been offered holiday homes, use of apartments and several invitations to stay with friends who live abroad.

VERY MUCH ALIVE

I mentioned to a great friend, David Kirby, how my aria adventure had fuelled my love of music and how important it had become in my life. Sooner than I could blink, he and the wonderful actress and producer Jo Kirkland were organising a music festival in my honour called Rejoice the Voice. They gave a huge amount of their time to organise a brilliant festival in Witley. All those who attended will agree that it was something very special.

More recently, my October tennis/golf touring mates have grouped together to help me buy my first wheelchair, a very flashy foldable electric number that will help me get out and about and keep me safe. I was genuinely very touched when Rich Crawford broached the idea with me.

My great friend Chris Guinness recorded an excellent cover of David Bowie's 'Heroes' and dedicated it to the MND community. It forms the backing track to the video for 50 Million Gin, a fundraising idea to thank those who campaigned for the government's recent £50 million funding pledge for more research into finding a cure for MND. It's a great gin and there's even a new signature cocktail – just visit 50milliongin.co.uk or google '50 Million Gin' to find out more. It was so kind and generous of Chris to think of doing this.

I've always maintained that you should try and make as many friends in life as you can. You never know when you're going to need them. Always look for the good in people and don't talk about them behind their backs, not least because what goes around comes around. Don't pretend to be anything other than who you are, including your failings. Never show off or brag, particularly about money and material possessions, and endeavour to be humble and a good listener.

I always try to make time for other people and make them feel good about themselves. For some of us, this comes naturally. Others, like me, have to work a little harder at it. I often get so wrapped up in my own world that I forget about others, but then I hopefully remember the truth of the old maxim that 'giving is so much more important than taking'.

Be generous in life. You will reap the rewards in so many ways.

Kindness

I'm now entering a hitherto unknown world to me – that of a 'disabled' person. Previously, I'd only ever picked up on the idea that this country is poor at looking after disabled people and often marginalises them. But thus far, my experience has been totally the opposite. I get looked after and am shown so much kindness that it makes me feel special.

This won't go down well with some of my fellow Chelsea fans, but I recently went to Anfield to watch a Liverpool match because this was definitely on my bucket list. The stewards, seeing that I was struggling a bit with my walking stick, ushered me in through a VIP entrance and then escorted me to a lift. At the top, the Liverpool supporters couldn't have been more helpful and accommodating, ensuring that I got to my seat safely. They say northerners are more friendly, and I can bear witness to this.

On another occasion, we went up to the Royal Albert Hall to watch some seniors Masters' tennis. We had bought cheap seats at the last minute, up in 'the gods', but we didn't care; we were there just to have some fun. On the other hand, I looked up at the steep climb to the seats with some trepidation, although I still thought I could manage. Duncan then had a word with a kindly looking steward to see if we could get moved a little lower. Ten minutes later, we found ourselves going down in the lift to court level, then being ushered into an empty private box! This had to be the upgrade of all time, from £28 seats to a box on sale for £2,750 (we googled it). My lovely friend Mel, who was with us, took the name of the steward and wrote a big thank you email to the Royal Albert Hall afterwards, which was a very kind and thoughtful thing to do.

This kind of thing is more the norm than the exception. Jess once phoned up a London theatre to see what the situation was with disabled tickets. We were given the Royal Box at no extra cost with its own private toilet and bar. What a treat! The staff at Chelsea FC are always brilliant at accommodating my requests for match tickets. And the Blue Badge parking scheme is wonderful – I no longer make catty comments about why there are always so many disabled spots in supermarket car parks taking up prime positions. It's brilliant and makes such a difference. Even the government gives me a weekly handout to help me with my costs!

In general, this country is full of caring people who naturally show kindness to those who need it. Whether it's being helped up from a chair or assistance with getting off a train, there's no shortage of people willing to help. Showing kindness and compassion in this world goes a long way. I receive it in abundance and am so grateful. It's truly heartwarming and makes me realise what's really important in life.

I want to end this chapter with a passage from an unknown author that perfectly sums up my feelings:

You came naked

You will leave naked

You came without anything

You will leave without anything

You arrived weak

You will leave weak

So, why so much hatred, resentment, envy, selfishness and pride?

We will all go empty handed, what all material things we have earned, we earned here, and will leave everything here only.

The only thing that will go with you, that you actually earned here is the love you shared, the compassion you showed, the humbleness, your gratitude, your helpfulness, your kindness.

That is the legacy you will leave here that everyone will follow.

Celebrating Chelsea's equaliser against Liverpool at Stamford Bridge

Rejoice the Voice Music Festival in aid of MND with great friend Mel

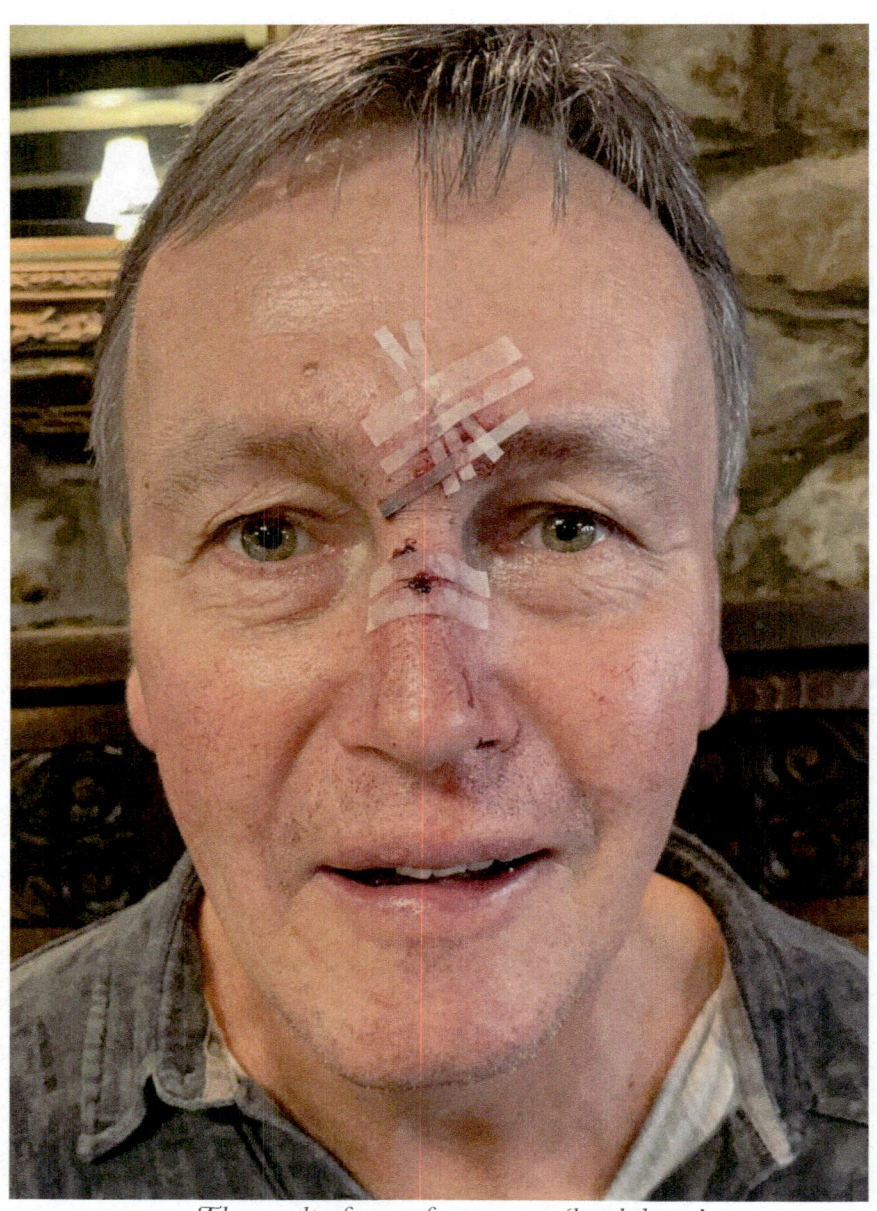

The result of one of my many 'headplants'

10

ASSISTED DYING

'To be, or not to be: that is the question:
Whether 'tis nobler in the mind to suffer
The slings and arrows of outrageous fortune,
Or to take arms against a sea of troubles,
And by opposing end them?'
Hamlet

Assisted dying, also referred to as assisted suicide or voluntary euthanasia, is a subject I feel very strongly about. It involves prescribing life-ending drugs for terminally ill, mentally competent adults to administer themselves after meeting strict legal safeguards. I am firmly in favour of legalising assisted dying in the UK.

It is a hugely controversial topic around the world. Legal and normalised in some countries while totally taboo in others, it is the focus of one of the key ethical debates of current times. Many believe that allowing a person who is terminally ill and in pain to pass away at a moment of their own choosing is morally right. Those opposed to the practice on religious, moral, and ethical grounds argue that nature must be allowed to take its course.

In the UK, the Assisted Dying Bill passed unopposed on 22nd October 2021 following a Second Reading debate in the House of Lords. There has, thankfully, been a dramatic shift of public opinion in the UK towards legalising the practice.

After the Bill was passed, Sarah Wootton, the chief executive of a campaigning charity called Dignity in Dying, summed the situation up beautifully:

'Mounting evidence is proving the ban on assisted dying to be uncompassionate, unequal and deeply unsafe. As evidenced in so many speeches today, none of us are protected from the suffering it can cause, including peers and their loved ones. We are pleased that attempts to frustrate this debate and wilfully mischaracterise what this Bill calls for were rightly withdrawn.

'This Assisted Dying Bill would bring much-needed choice, compassion and protection to terminally ill people. It would protect families from making the impossible choice between breaking the law or watching a loved one suffer. It would enable healthcare professionals to offer the full range of options their patients want. It would finally bring this 60-year-old law into the 21st century, making the UK a world-leader on end-of-life choice.'

I fully support the bill. For me, it's all about empowering people to take control of their lives and deaths, to give them and their families dignity in death and, of course, to end unnecessary pain and suffering. Its potential to transform all our lives and deaths for the better is colossal.

I don't think for one minute that I personally would go down the euthanasia route, but you never know. Despite my hard exterior and positive mindset, I am soft on the inside. I'm beginning to struggle with the difficulties and frustrations of my disability, and I face a very uncertain future. I just want to have this option available to me should I need it.

To know I had the power to choose this dignified way to end my life would be a great comfort to me, like an insurance policy. It would give me peace of mind and enable me to live better in the present, free from fear and anxiety.

Recently, I asked my three children whether they would support me in a decision to end my life if my suffering, both physical and mental, became unbearable. All three said yes. It would be a win-win for everyone concerned. I wouldn't have to suffer, and my family wouldn't have to endure watching me do it. Ultimately, I believe, they would respect me for taking this difficult decision, for being proactive and taking control of the end of my life, just as I have throughout the rest of it.

I love the eulogy that M delivers for James Bond at the end of No Time To Die. 'The proper function of man is to live, not to exist. I shall not waste my days in trying to prolong them. I shall use my time.' That sums up my attitude to life and death perfectly.

VERY MUCH ALIVE

What would the alternative to assisted suicide be if things were to get bad enough for me? I'd continue existing but not living. I'd be in pain, anxious and depressed. And I'd be a financial and emotional burden on my family – something I never want to be. Not surprisingly, for many, the alternative turns out to be suicide.

According to Dignity in Dying, 300 people with terminal illnesses commit suicide in England each year. The current law is forcing those who are going to die soon anyway to risk painful and gruesome deaths. In the absence of an assisted dying law, they are resorting to taking their lives behind closed doors, with all the trauma to themselves and their loved ones that entails. And if their thoughts are turning in that direction, they are unable to have an open conversation about it with their doctors or families. To even discuss the possibility of suicide with someone could implicate them in a crime punishable by a prison sentence of up to 14 years.

How cruel it is to force terminally ill people to consider suicide as the only way to relieve their suffering. How awful it must be if a suicide attempt fails. I read about one MND sufferer who was considering throwing himself down the stairs in his wheelchair and another who was contemplating starving himself to death. This is so wrong and inhumane. The case to legalise assisted dying could not be clearer, in my opinion.

Let's look at some facts (sourced from Dignity in Dying):

- 84% of people in the UK support the right to assisted dying for the terminally ill.
- 100 million people in North America have access to assisted dying.
- 44% of people would break the law to assist a loved one to die and risk 14 years in prison.
- 80% of religious people support an assisted dying law.
- 86% of people with a disability support a change to the law.

To my mind, those who oppose the legalisation of assisted dying have not come up with any compelling, logical or persuasive reasons that in any way outweigh the case for a change in the law. In fact, some of their arguments seem quite shallow to me.

In a recent ITV documentary called Dying with Dignity? a medical professional who is opposed to the legalisation of assisted dying tried to argue that it's palliative care that needs to be improved in the UK, not the laws of the land. This annoyed me greatly. Palliative care here is already excellent and only marginal improvements can be made. Even then, there is a limit to how much pain relief can be provided without actually killing the patient, which is exactly what the opponents of the Assisted Dying Bill are not prepared to contemplate. Are we really going to argue that people must be kept alive just so they can suffer? Try telling that to someone in agony with terminal cancer.

VERY MUCH ALIVE

I asked my daughter Jo, who has just finished six years of medical training, to comment on how she felt the medical profession currently views the debate. She said, 'This completely depends on the person's own beliefs. There's no one unanimous opinion among doctors as a whole. It's a very complex topic!! But not one that I've discussed with a lot of other doctors, so I can't say for sure what the majority opinion is.' I believe the medical profession is beginning to appreciate the genuine compassionate benefits that assisted dying will bring to patients. It is however sometimes at odds with their 'cure at all costs' training and hippocratic oath, so tends not to be widely debated.

Religious people sometimes oppose assisted dying on the grounds that miracles can happen. Occasionally, a person with a terminal illness does recover, but it's very rare, and this argument ignores the suffering that all the others have to go through. Another common religious argument is that only God should have the power to determine when a person dies. My answer to this is, 'If there is a God, he certainly seems to leave the big decisions in life up to us. Would you say only God should have the power to decide whether someone who has fallen into a canal gets rescued or not? How exactly would that be supposed to work out?'

Others point out that states of mind can be temporary and that many people have failed in suicide attempts but gone on to lead fulfilling lives. This is no doubt true, but it seems to me to be clutching at straws to use it as grounds for opposing the legalisation of voluntary euthanasia. You could use the same logic to argue against marriage. After all, some people have lived to regret that too!

Perhaps the most common reason for opposing assisted dying is the 'slippery slope' argument. This claims that if voluntary euthanasia was legalised, vulnerable people might be pressured into ending their lives when they didn't really want to. It's more than reasonable to ask where changes in the law might lead and to be concerned about their possible effects on vulnerable people. But unscrupulous people can already put pressure on others to end their lives. I believe we should work to ensure that there is minimal scope for abuse rather than denying suffering people the fundamental right to choose whether to live or die. And in the UK, we have the best lawyers and legal system in the world to provide the necessary safeguards.

I accept that a change to legalise assisted dying is not easy on many levels, but that does not detract from the fact that the vast majority of people, not just those with terminal illnesses, are in favour of a change in the law. For me, the pros massively outweigh the cons. It will not be an easy transition and mistakes will be made, but the big picture is that legalising assisted dying in the UK would lead to a more compassionate and caring society and greatly help to improve the lives of terminally ill people.

I look forward to seeing how the Assisted Dying Bill progresses. I am hopeful that we will get the right outcome

VERY MUCH ALIVE

because, thankfully, we live in a country where public opinion is listened to.

11

MY BATTLE WITH MND

'Death is more universal than life; everyone dies but not everyone lives.'
Andrew Sachs

Responding to a life-threatening diagnosis is quite binary – you either passively let it kill you, or you fight it. You won't be surprised to hear that I go for Option B. For me, it's actually more of a war than a battle. My enemy is, of course, MND, and we're both playing the long game. There are many fights, confrontations and skirmishes, and I try to win as many of them as possible, never giving in or raising the white flag.

This approach is a really effective coping mechanism for me. I've learned it not only from Rob Burrow but also from Doddie Weir, another inspirational former rugby international with MND, this time from the Union rather than the League form of the sport.

If I trip and fall over and smack my head on the floor, MND has won that particular battle. If I trip and stay on my feet, I'm the winner. If I go for a walk without a stick and come back unscathed, that's another victory chalked up to me.

I fall over pretty regularly, probably two or three times a month, mainly because I'm a bit cavalier with my attitude. I'm a risk-taker by nature, and I generally resist using safety aids like sticks or wheelchairs. I have become quite adept at falling 'well' – I've had plenty of practice, after all – but I do often injure myself. Spraining a wrist or injuring a shoulder are common injuries for me, as are bumps on the head. I hate it when these things happen, not because they hurt but because they mean that MND has won those little skirmishes and set me back. It's bad enough not being able to use your legs properly, but that means relying on your arms more, and having a sprained wrist does not help with that one bit.

One of Doddie's favourites sayings is, 'If you don't use it, you lose it'. How very true that is. That's the attitude I take to walking, and I'm taking it to eating, too. I am resisting getting a feeding tube, known as a PEG (percutaneous endoscopic gastrostomy – why do doctors like these long Latin words?), inserted into my belly, although everyone tells me I should. I don't want a foreign body attached to my stomach, thanks very much. I want to enjoy eating and drinking via the correct orifice for as long as possible, even if this means the odd choking episode. When I do have the PEG inserted, I will have surrendered some more ground in the fight against MND.

VERY MUCH ALIVE

It's a similar story with driving. My family are trying to get me to give it up, but I feel I can still drive as well as, if not better than, the majority of other road users, so I'm holding out for as long as possible. I don't want to lose my independence and give up more territory to the enemy. Of course, if I felt I was putting myself, passengers or other road users in any danger, I would stop at once.

I have a wheelchair and a power scooter (both great fun), but I avoid using them as much as possible, preferring to keep going with what I've got left in my legs, even if this means I walk incredibly slowly. If I don't use it, I'll lose it. My personal trainer Ed – the smiley one - comes to my house twice a week and puts me through a rigorous and painful routine of stretches and balancing and strengthening exercises. After each session, I feel great and more determined to fight the next battle with renewed vigour. It's like a battleground training camp.

Whenever I go out for a meal, I always make a mental note on the way in of where the toilets are, as I often need to get to them quickly (bladder weakness is a side effect of MND). Recently, I was having lunch with some friends in a smart London restaurant, and when I arrived, I found they were on the far side of the room.

You can probably guess where this story is heading, but there's another element to it too. My mouth muscles are very weak these days, especially my tongue and lips. This means that whenever I take a drink, I have to have a napkin or tissue ready to wipe up the liquid that dribbles out. Invariably, I can't catch it all. At home, I always wear an adult bib, but not so when I'm out.

On this occasion, a lot of red wine is drunk, and I have a white shirt on (in hindsight, not the best colour to have chosen). Slowly but surely, a lot of wine finds its way onto it. Then I get a signal that I need a wee. I have to get to the toilets as quickly as possible, which is not always easy at the speed I walk, but I seem to make it to the urinals in time and stand in front of one. This is where the problems begin. I'm losing sensation in my fingers and my fine motor skills are deserting me, so I fumble at my belt, but I can neither release the button on my light blue jeans nor find the zip catch. Then I feel a slow trickle of warmth going down my right leg – clearly, I am dressed to the right on this particular day. Once it starts, I cannot stop it.

I look at myself in the mirror. I've never been a great one for taking care of my appearance anyway, but this is pretty bad. I appear to have been shot in the chest, and there's no hiding the fact that one of my legs is light coloured and the other one dark. I have two options: I either give up and go home, or I do the walk of shame back through the restaurant.

I already get a lot of stares, anyway, because the spasticity in my legs makes me walk in a jilted robotic fashion, but this time I really am going to be quite a spectacle. What course of action should I take? Welcome to my world.

Naturally, I'm not prepared to lose this little battle to the enemy, so I make my way back through the restaurant with a broad smile on my face, engaging the eye of everyone who stares at me. Then I resume enjoying my meal. The jeans dry out, I put a jumper on and all's well that ends well. Victory is mine today.

With that little anecdote out of the way, I'm going to turn to an even nastier side effect of MND. The issue in question is bowel movements. We've already discussed bladder weakness, but unfortunately, MND affects the other side of human plumbing as well.

Naturally, it's extremely unpleasant for all concerned when things go wrong in this department. You may say, well, just prepare better; when you start to feel the urge, get to the nearest toilet quickly. But it doesn't actually work that way – you go from no urge to a very urgent urge within seconds. Maybe a clever doctor can explain why that is. You may also think 'TMI' ('too much information'), but I feel it's important for people to appreciate the practical and psychological challenges that people with this and other diseases have to deal with.

To be honest, I have not found a solution or coping mechanism for this particular dilemma yet. But generally speaking, I'm winning the war on the mental side. The one thing MND doesn't take away from you is your mind – it can't affect your attitude, unlike other neurological diseases like dementia. My mind is as strong and sharp as ever.

Sometimes, when I'm sitting still or laying in bed, I can't believe anything is wrong with me at all. And at the end of a recent long flight, two air hostesses came over to help me get out of my seat. At first, I had no idea what they were trying to do – I thought they might have been attempting to arrest me! I had completely forgotten about my disease. It's only when I try to move that I remember.

There's a great Sunday Times best-selling book by Dr Kathryn Mannix called With the End in Mind: Dying, Death and Wisdom in an Age of Denial. Kathryn has studied and practised palliative care for 30 years. She explains:

'People are not limited so much by their illness as by their attitude to it. The illness may present physical challenges, but the emotional challenge is often far more important. Our human spirit may stumble as the path ahead appears too daunting, yet with support and encouragement, our resilience can be re-enabled and used to find creative solutions.'

I made my mind up very early after my diagnosis that, however badly MND affected me, I would never complain or moan about it. That would be handing a little victory to the illness. It would also create a negative mindset for me and the people around me. Refraining from complaining has turned out to be a great coping mechanism, which helps me stay strong and focused. On the odd occasion when I do get a little low or unhappy, I try to snap out of it as quickly as possible. I tell myself it's the enemy trying to ambush me and quickly take evasive action.

Everyone with a life-threatening condition should take responsibility for finding the best ways to cope and stay strong. Of course, you should listen to the advice that many well-intentioned people will give you, but you need to be discerning about it. You have to find solutions that work best for you and keep experimenting until you get it right. No one else can do this for you.

You may even find that living with a terminal disease can be better than all right. If you accept it and approach it with the right attitude, the end of life can be profoundly liberating. Look at it this way – if you're like 99% of the population, it's something you've always been dreading, at least beneath the surface. Now you're finally face to face with it, you don't have to dread it anymore. And as I've tried to emphasise throughout this book, there can be magical side effects, such as more love in your life and increased appreciation for the things that really matter. But as Rob Burrow says in the quote I used for the Introduction, you have to look for them. 'You have to seek the wonderful in life, it won't come knocking at your door'.

Another great book I've read about the end of life is Philip Gould's When I Die: Lessons from the Death Zone. Philip was a key strategist in the Labour Party revival which brought Tony Blair to power in 1997, and he died of cancer aged 61. I want to quote a few passages from his book because they sum up so well the positive things that can happen at the end of someone's life.

'Death is usually depicted as a time of decline, of growing irrelevance, as the ending of growth, the cessation of contribution. To some extent those things may be true. But for the dying themselves, like me, there is another dynamic at work: the sheer intensity of death leads us to assess our world in ways we have never done before, each contributing to a kind of pre-death moment of judgement'.

'The unvarnished certainty that you are going to die within a certain period of time is an immensely powerful thing. It provides the opportunity for fulfilment and the experience of extraordinary depths of feeling and the chance of reconciliation that would never otherwise occur'.

'. . . a respected consultant psychiatrist . . . said two things to me that affected me deeply. The first was that the only way to have a good death is to accept it. The second was to understand that for many people, if not most, death is the most important time of life'.

'Death is not frightening if you accept it. It is a time for immense change and transformation, a time to fulfil yourself and others, and a chance in a small way to change the world'.

I feel incredibly lucky to have found ways of making my end of life such a positive and fulfilling experience. My perspective has changed, and I've become detached from the everyday stresses and worries that used to dominate my thinking as I plotted a course through life. All the trivial irritations have become irrelevant because bigger forces are at play. It's almost as if you reach a higher level of consciousness. I sometimes feel like I'm on a different, more privileged level than everyone else, and this is an ordinary bloke from Surrey talking, not some enlightened yogi!

I recently re-read a book that I first read about 20 years ago, long before I was diagnosed with MND. It's called Don't Sweat the Small Stuff… and It's All Small Stuff by Richard Carlson. I consider it one of the best self-help books I've ever read. It's short but full of gems, like:

'Being listened to and heard is one of the greatest desires of the human heart. And those who learn to listen are the most loved and respected. Those who are in the habit of correcting others are often resented and avoided'.

'A wonderful, heartfelt strategy for becoming more peaceful and loving is to practice allowing others the joy of being right—give them the glory'.

'The quality of patience goes a long way toward your goal of creating a more peaceful and loving self. The more patient you are, the more accepting you will be of what is, rather than insisting that life be exactly as you would like it to be. Without patience, life is extremely frustrating. You are easily annoyed, bothered, and irritated. Patience adds a dimension of ease and acceptance to your life. It's essential for inner peace'.

Well, I'm doing my best to follow his advice to be a better listener and more patient. I'm nearly five years into my

VERY MUCH ALIVE

diagnosis – my progression is slow, but this is a double-edged sword as it means my years of decline will also be slow. The war is still in its infancy, and I will have many more difficult battles to fight. I'm continuing to treat every situation as a new challenge to be overcome, which is how I cope best, but it's getting harder. Even simple things, like putting on socks, are now very difficult. It's a period of huge adjustment, not just for me but also for the rest of my family, especially Jess. It's not easy at times, but I'm as determined as ever to stay strong and carry on waging the battle.

12
THE LAST BIG TABOO

'Fear of death is ridiculous, because as long as you are not dead you are alive, and when you are dead there is nothing more to worry about!'
Paramahansa Yogananda (Indian Hindu monk)

Death is an uncomfortable topic, rarely discussed. Most of us don't want to talk about it or plan for it. I think a major reason for this is that we know, on some level, that if we did these things, we'd be forced to accept the reality of the situation – that death is inevitable. So instead, we choose to tiptoe around the subject until it's too late.

Our reluctance to talk about death and dying risks leaving us vulnerable and underprepared. The uncomfortable truth is this – while we can avoid talking about it, we can't avoid the thing itself, whether our own deaths or those of others.

Why is talking about death such a taboo?
- Fear of the unknown. Many people are afraid of death. Some are afraid of dying alone. Others fear pain and

suffering. Most of us don't know how or when death will happen, so we just ignore it. We focus on what life has to offer and block out the inevitable.
- Fear of saying the wrong thing. It's not only family members and friends who find death difficult to discuss. The dying themselves often find themselves struggling to express their thoughts and feelings about the subject. We don't want to make matters worse for others, so we choose to say nothing at all.
- Fear of being a burden. Many terminally ill people choose to avoid the topic of death out of fear of causing pain to family members and friends. They are concerned about how their deaths will affect those they will be leaving behind and don't want to add anything to the long list of things they already have to worry about, so they don't bring up the subject. They may also fear, consciously or unconsciously, that if they talk openly about their feelings their loved ones may reject them. This isn't surprising in a society that avoids the topic of dying like the plague.

If we learned more about death and discussed it openly, I believe we would learn to accept it as a fact of life. We would free ourselves up to lead enriching, fulfilling lives without being so fearful of their inevitable ending. People need to get comfortable with death. It is not a failure – it's a part of life.

VERY MUCH ALIVE

How do we initiate change and open up the conversation about death and dying? To some extent, this is happening already, albeit slowly. Events like the Covid pandemic, the threat of climate change and the war in Ukraine have brought the subject into our consciousnesses in a way we just can't ignore. And in general, we're becoming better as a society at expressing emotion and talking about difficult and uncomfortable topics.

It's good to see the Death Cafe movement blossoming. There's also a welcome growth in something I haven't mentioned before, which is the End of Life Doula movement. A death doula is someone who supports people through the dying process. According to the International End of Life Doula Association, they 'help restore sacredness to dying, provide respite to exhausted caregivers, bring deep meaning to the dying experience, and prepare people for the last breaths of their loved one'. They have been described as midwives (or husbands) of death, which is a role that makes perfect sense to me. If we have specialists to see us through one end of life, why not the other one too?

Aura's Facebook group, Death Chat, is also playing its part in opening up the conversation about death and dying. But as a society, we need to do more. The media has an important role to play in this process. There needs to be a change in the way death is described and reported on. Replacing the old-fashioned and solemn word 'obituary' with 'life story' would be a good start . . .

VERY MUCH ALIVE

One of my favourite TV programmes is Sports Personality of the Year, otherwise known as SPOTY. I don't think I've missed one edition in the last 50 years, and 2021 was no exception. It was heartwarming to hear gymnast Simone Biles talk openly about her mental health struggles and the support she received when her problems surfaced after the Tokyo Olympics. You could tell she was now in a much better place because she had been able to open up and talk about her issues.

There was also a segment with the beaming British diver Tom Daley talking about how delighted he was to be married to his husband and how thrilled he was to have a child. Mental health issues and being gay are now openly discussed – the taboos have been lifted. I'm confident that the same will happen over time with death and dying. But we're not there yet.

At the end of SPOTY came the part where the sports people who had died during the past year were remembered. The lights were lowered, voices were hushed, and a very serious-looking Alex Scott started using phrases like 'sadly say goodbye' and 'remembering many loved ones who have sadly departed'. (Why use euphemisms? Where have these people departed to? They have died. Why not say so?) Then the most melancholic violin music imaginable started up before the roll call of deceased sports people began.

What happened next was totally juxtaposed with what had been said before. It featured the likes of Saint and

VERY MUCH ALIVE

Greavsie (former footballers and pundits Ian St John and Jimmy Greaves) having a right old laugh and racing commentator Murray Walker having a ding-dong with Nigel Mansell. These were all sports people who had had fantastic and successful careers, and there was so much to celebrate about their lives. The vast majority had also lived out their natural lifespans.

Was I sad when I heard that Murray Walker had died? To be honest, not really. I just remember him as a fantastic character who had brought Formula 1 races to life. He had a wonderful career travelling the world on the F1 circuit, then he died at the grand old age of 97. Not exactly a tragedy.

It would have been so much better if Alex Scott had said something like, 'We now celebrate the wonderful lives and achievements of the sports people who died this year', followed by some more upbeat music. I'm not asking for Cliff Richard's Congratulations, just something a bit more inspiring than the depressing violin music. It would be so good if the BBC changed the tone at this year's ceremony. I will be watching carefully!

I've discussed previously how the archaic funeral industry needs to modernise and offer funerals that are less sombre and black. I know of three funeral companies that are already doing this, but there are no doubt many more. Exit Here in Chiswick state they will 'create a personalised and life-affirming funeral that's right for you'. They also hold weekly open house coffee mornings. Poetic Endings in southeast London say that they 'create funerals that honour, heal, and inspire' and 'empower you to have the funeral that you want and need'. The Modern Funeral in Brighton's tagline is 'Simple. Meaningful. Honest'. It's great to see these companies trying to be different and more death-positive. And there are hosts of online businesses, including Aura, that are helping to provide better, more tailored and meaningful funerals. So the industry is changing for the better, albeit slowly.

The medical profession also needs to do end of life better. Even Jess admits this. Medics, as good as they are, can be too prescriptive and focused on finding a cure at all costs. This sometimes ignores the emotional needs of the patient. Carolyn Hornblow writes:

'We, the healthcare professionals, see death more than anyone else. We must stop the silence and start to illuminate and teach the public that death is not the fearsome monster that ignorance and fear create but can be a gentle release and a gift if fears are addressed and intimacy encouraged. Intimacy of family and friends can be increased as discussion of issues of death and dying occur, allowing more honesty, closeness and vulnerability to replace silence and avoidance of the issue.

'Currently in the healthcare industry, there is a habit of giving negative news and information in a minimised way. The inference is that if you just get the facts out and then talk positively about what wonderful things medicine can do, then the patient will go away feeling reassured and you, the doctor, will also feel better because you gave the patient negative news in a positive way'.

I was heartened when I asked my daughter Jo, who has recently qualified to be a doctor, about how much training she got to support people emotionally at the end of their lives and break bad news to them. This was her response:

'We had multiple role play and teaching sessions throughout medical school and as junior doctors. They teach us how to communicate effectively and sensitively in difficult situations. Good communication to a patient is arguably just as good as prescribing them medication. We had a module that was dedicated to palliative care teaching, where we went into hospices and palliative care wards.'

I sense doctors are better nowadays at looking at more holistic ways to treat patients and better address their emotional needs. People at the end of their lives don't just want drugs to alleviate symptoms. They want to be talked and listened to and to express their feelings.

For the record, I would like to affirm that I've had exemplary care from the NHS since my MND diagnosis, managed by hardworking, dedicated people who are generally underpaid and undervalued. I've seen first-hand how much stress and pressure doctors are put under by an ever more demanding public. For all the criticism levelled at the NHS, I believe there is no better comparable service anywhere in the world. As a result of my various mishaps and accidents abroad, I've experienced other healthcare institutions whose standards fall a long way short of those of the NHS.

I believe people are gradually waking up to the benefits of the things I have been discussing in this book – talking about death more openly and making plans for send- offs that truly reflect them as people. There is a massive shift taking place in the UK in terms of the type of funerals people are having. I firmly believe that in 10 years' time, direct cremations will be a more popular choice than traditional funerals. Hopefully, we can get to the point where we celebrate death just as fully as we celebrate life.

The last big societal taboo is slowly being broken. It will still take time, but people like me are beginning to realise that you can live better by accepting your mortality, talking about death and not fearing it.

EPILOGUE: THE ROAD AHEAD

'No one wants to die. Even people who want to go to heaven don't want to die to get there. And yet, death is the destination we all share. No one has ever escaped it, and that is how it should be, because death is very likely the single best invention of life. It's life's change agent. It clears out the old to make way for the new.'
Steve Jobs

Here I am, five years on from my MND diagnosis, and once again I'm feeling extremely lucky.

There are two main reasons for this. First, my deterioration due to the illness has been slow and is predicted to stay that way. During this period, I've seen several other MND patients lose their battles with the disease, many of them people who were diagnosed after me. For a few years now, I've regularly been meeting up with three other MND sufferers of around my age to share experiences and offer each other advice. Our group of four has recently become two. I witness the rapid decline that occurs in the vast majority of cases and wonder why I wasn't dealt the same hand. Like so many things in life, it just seems so random.

I'm often asked if my positive attitude has made a difference to how my MND has progressed. I honestly don't think so. I look at the likes of Doddie Weir and Rob Burrow, who are both younger than me and were diagnosed later. They are two of the most optimistic and determined people you're ever likely to meet, yet their illnesses have progressed much faster than mine. So I can't attribute the fact that I'm still alive and kicking to the power of thinking positively, or offer any magic formula for living longer after a terminal diagnosis. What I can try to do is demonstrate that, however long you have left, taking a positive approach allows you to make the most of it. And express my gratitude for the 'extra time' I have been granted.

It's been a tremendous privilege to have this time to contemplate my death. Many people never get this opportunity. Around a quarter of all deaths are sudden, with no warning. Some people say they would like to die in the night without knowing anything about it, but I'm definitely not one of them. I'm incredibly glad I've had the chance to prepare for my end of life properly.

That brings me to the second, more important, reason why I feel lucky. Since my diagnosis, I've had the most incredible, memorable and rewarding five years of my life. So much so that if you offered me the chance to rewind to a point before I developed MND and then carry on without it ever happening, I genuinely don't think I would take it.

A big part of what has made the last five years so magical has been the people around me. I have been the recipient of so much heartfelt love and kindness that I feel truly blessed. It has been touching and humbling, and I've connected with family and friends like never before. I've got to see the really good parts of human nature, the compassionate and caring sides, and experienced first-hand how well British society caters for those in need.

Other 'miraculous' elements of my past few years have been more inner. My outlook on life has changed completely. I don't get as stressed and anxious as before, and I don't sweat the small stuff. I have somehow developed an inner confidence I never previously had. I feel far less self-conscious than I used to, even though I'm regularly doing things like spilling wine down my shirt and falling over. I really don't worry what other people think of me anymore. I am who I am, and I can't change that. I'm not being arrogant here. I think it's to do with the bigger issues at play. I'm in the twilight of my very good life. I've been there, done that, and have no more to prove to anyone. In short, I've found some inner peace.

Quite a lot of this book, one way or another, has been about losing my voice. I have been mute, non-verbal, speechless, or however you want to describe it, for over two years now, and recently I've begun to wonder whether this has actually contributed to my inner tranquillity and improved mental wellbeing. I can certainly find myself remarkably contented when not able to be part of a conversation. I watch people getting more and more stressed as they struggle to get themselves heard and feel well off out of it. Sometimes I'm happy to be on the sideline as an observer and content just to listen.

I did some research as to why Buddhist monks take the vow of silence. Paradoxically, in the Buddhist tradition, this is considered the route to proper speech. They call it 'speaking with silence'.

- By refraining from revealing whatever comes to mind, the monks in question avoid saying anything negative. This is a way of practising nonviolence.
- They believe that silence strengthens your spirituality by giving you an opportunity to be present within yourself. If you don't verbally engage with others, you are compelled to interact with your own thoughts. As a result, you will tend to understand yourself better.
- Observing a vow of silence also promotes listening abilities. It's easier to hear others out if you can't interrupt them and listening helps you progress along the path to enlightenment.
- Silence helps keep the mind quiet. This is a major step towards achieving inner peace and the goal of meditation. When the mind is freed from wild thoughts, you have more control over what you think.
- The monks believe that a vow of silence will help them to develop self-love. This in turn will help them cultivate compassion towards others. It is difficult to have this attitude when you do not love yourself.

VERY MUCH ALIVE

I can't fully attribute my own inner peace and contentment to my own enforced silence, but I do firmly believe that by bringing me in tune with the Buddhist monks who choose not to speak, it has been a big contributing factor. In the near future, I want to explore how much more meditation may be able to help me continue on this path of improved mental wellbeing, inner calmness and better perspective on life.

Another thing that MND has forced me to do is not rush everything so much. I used to spend my entire life hurtling along at breakneck speed. I can't do that anymore. This is partly because my body won't allow me to, but also because I'm reliant on other people doing things for me on their terms and at their own speed. This can be frustrating, but I've learnt to draw a deep breath and just accept that everything I do is going to take longer. In the grand scheme of things, if this makes me late or I miss a train, it's no big deal. I believe slowing down has helped me, as I feel less stressed and anxious than before. I realise there are things I can't control, so I go with the flow.

On the other hand, I know that life is going to get harder in the coming years as my health deteriorates, not just for me but also for my family, especially Jess. They have to act as my carers for much of the time, and it can be hard for me to communicate what I want or need, which is frustrating for me and difficult for them. Patience is required on both sides.

I accept I often appear withdrawn and in my own little world. I find myself concentrating so much on coping with the effects of my disease that I can forget the feelings of others, for whom the situation is also difficult. I probably have to work harder on getting the balance right.

I view the future with some trepidation and unease, but also with excitement, because I'm optimistic about the opportunities my new circumstances will afford me. My biggest challenge is to keep myself mentally strong. Life isn't always easy for me, and although I project a hard exterior, I do have 'down' periods and they are becoming more frequent. But I just take this as evidence that I have to work harder at finding better coping mechanisms and ways to maintain positivity.

I have fully accepted my mortality and the fact that life is finite. I firmly believe that there is no afterlife. You don't, in my opinion, move on to some other realm of existence. Instead, in the words of Belinda Carlisle, 'Heaven is a Place on Earth'. Your memories and legacy continue in this world. I will live on through my children – who are half me, after all – and in my children's children. And also in the minds of everyone who knew me and who I've had some connection with.

My theory is that you have two lives: your bodily one, which ends when you die, and your spiritual one, which continues on for a very long time. It's important for me to leave this spiritual legacy – that is my heaven. I want to know that during my lifetime I've done my bit to make a net improvement to society and humanity as a whole. I love the old Irish saying, 'You die twice: once when you take your last breath, and the second time when the last person speaks your name for the last time'.

If, by some miracle, I do go to heaven and eternal life, I will be livid! It's been hard enough to navigate my time on earth, I really don't want to have to do that again for all eternity. My eternity is here, while I'm still alive.

I loved this poem, read at my uncle's recent funeral, which reminds us that what really matters is our time on planet earth:

Not, how did he die, but how did he live?
Not, what did he gain, but what did he give?
These are the units to measure the worth
Of a man as a man, regardless of his birth

Nevertheless, despite the "Not how did he die" bit, I am determined to have a 'good death'. That phrase probably means different things to different people, but here's what it means to me:

I want to die at home, not in some sanitised institution like a hospice or hospital, which is currently where over 50% of people end their lives (I find that figure shocking). I want to be in my own bedroom with my family and dogs all over me, licking my face. Or the dogs, anyway! As I've stated in my End of Life Wishes page on Aura, I would like relaxing piano music to be playing and a lavender infuser to be perfuming the air. And I emphatically do not wish to be pumped full of debilitating drugs like morphine. I want

VERY MUCH ALIVE

to remain as aware of what's happening as possible, even if I'm in some pain. In short, I plan to be as happy in death as I have been in life and to go out with a smile on my face.

After I've died, I don't want to be rushed off in a coffin to some mortuary. I want to stay at home for a few days to give a chance for my family and friends to say goodbye. If this idea freaks them out, they needn't worry. The body does not start deteriorating or decomposing until about day three or four.

I realise that things may not work out exactly as I have outlined above, but there's no harm in asking for what you want! Don't get me wrong, though; I have no intention of dying any time soon. Far from it. Life still has so much to offer. However, I accept that nothing lasts forever. The end will come for me in the not-too-distant future, just as it will for all of us. We've only been given this amazing gift of life for a brief window of time. In the meantime, I'm very much alive!

Story Terrace

Printed in Great Britain
by Amazon